From Your Friends at **The MAILBOX®**

Themes To Grow On
Spring & Summer

Table Of Contents

Managing Editor: Susan Walker

Editor at Large: Diane Badden

Contributing Writers: Bonnie Cave, Judy Huskins, Sandy McNeil

Copy Editors: Tazmen Carlisle, Amy Kirtley-Hill, Karen L. Mayworth, Kristy Parton, Debbie Shoffner, Cathy Edwards Simrell

Cover Artists: Nick Greenwood, Ivy L. Koonce

Artists: Jennifer Tipton Bennett, Cathy S. Bruce, Theresa Lewis Goode, Donna K. Teal

The Mailbox® Books.com: Jennifer Tipton Bennett (DESIGNER/ARTIST); Stuart Smith (PRODUCTION ARTIST); Karen White (INTERNET COORDINATOR); Paul Fleetwood, Xiaoyun Wu (SYSTEMS)

President, The Mailbox Book Company™: Joseph C. Bucci

Director of Book Planning and Development: Chris Poindexter

Curriculum Director: Karen P. Shelton

Book Development Managers: Cayce Guiliano, Elizabeth H. Lindsay, Thad McLaurin

Editorial Planning: Kimberley Bruck (MANAGER); Debra Liverman, Sharon Murphy, Susan Walker (TEAM LEADERS)

Editorial and Freelance Management: Karen A. Brudnak; Sarah Hamblet, Hope Rodgers (EDITORIAL ASSISTANTS)

Editorial Production: Lisa K. Pitts (TRAFFIC MANAGER); Lynette Dickerson (TYPE SYSTEMS); Mark Rainey (TYPESETTER)

Librarian: Dorothy C. McKinney

How To Use This Book

This book is a collection of weekly thematic units that successfully incorporate the use of hands-on, across-the-curriculum activities. *Themes To Grow On* focuses on 19 weekly thematic units.

Each unit includes five sections: math, language arts, science, social studies, and art. Each of these sections contains a variety of teacher-tested learning activities that can be done individually, in small groups, or in a whole-group setting. A snack idea and a culminating activity are also provided. For each theme, there are two reproducibles with suggestions for their use. By combining the activities and ideas in each unit, you can create a week filled with learning, discovery, and fun.

Using themes that interest children facilitates learning. *Themes To Grow On* is a collection of carefully developed thematic units that will spark children's interest and meet your specific needs as an educator. This book is filled with teacher-tested ideas that balance developmentally appropriate activities with basic skills practice.

Activities in centers often focus on a specific theme and are used to integrate the curriculum. Because learning centers are an important part of a youngster's school experience, suggestions for utilizing themes in centers are given in each unit. Effective management of centers should allow children both free choice and guided exploration.

Suggestions For Enhancing
Themes To Grow On Units In Your Classroom

Here are some general ideas to enhance these units and assist you in incorporating thematic units in your classroom.

- Incorporate special guest speakers and parents, and plan field trips that are appropriate for each theme. Ideas for speakers and field trips are included in some of the units.

- Include fingerplays, poems, creative dramatics, chants, games, snacks, and cooking projects in your weekly theme.

- Be creative! Use special theme-related decorations to add to the excitement in your classroom. Fill your classroom with centers, books, posters, pictures, bulletin boards, and household items that lend themselves to the weekly theme. Have students dress up for certain theme day celebrations. Have a theme table on which to display special theme items brought in by you or your students.

- Ask for and encourage input from your students. They will have fun learning about what interests them. Find out what it is about each theme that they would like to do or learn about, and include it in your weekly unit.

- Celebrate! Have special theme parties. Allow your youngsters to assist in the planning and organizing of the parties!

Famous Americans

America—where you are free to be a doctor, lawyer, or teacher. What will your children grow up to be? This salute to famous Americans will inspire and inform your youngsters as they venture through a variety of learning activities.

MATH

Sally Ride

Sally Ride was the first American woman to travel in space. Ask your children to pretend they are astronauts getting ready to blast off into space. Tell them to squat down on the floor and count backwards from ten to one. Then let them blast off by jumping up into the air.

Abraham Lincoln

Abraham Lincoln, our sixteenth president, carried important papers, notes, and bills in his stovepipe hat. Have your children name other items that could have fit in President Lincoln's hat. Next have your youngsters sequentially name objects that would fit individually in other containers such as a thimble, a teacup, a shoebox, and a bathtub. Make a list of each set of objects.

Johnny Appleseed

John Chapman, who was also known as Johnny Appleseed, planted apple orchards and supplied pioneer families with young apple tree seedlings. Place a bag of apples in a learning center. Tell the children in the center to arrange the apples in a line from the smallest to the largest.

Roberto Clemente

Roberto Clemente was the first Latin American to be elected to the Baseball Hall Of Fame. He won four National League batting titles and in 1966 was voted the league's Most Valuable Player. Clemente also played in 12 All-Star games and helped his team, the Pittsburgh Pirates, win the World Series in 1960 and 1971. Let each child in a small group play an indoor version of baseball. Prepare for the activity by drawing a baseball diamond on a sheet of tagboard to create a gameboard. Place the gameboard in the center of the playing area. Put a set of math fact cards in the center of the diamond. Give each child a milk cap to use as a marker. Tell one child to place her marker on home plate. Have her remove the first card from the stack and give the answer to the math problem. If she is correct, she may advance to first base and repeat the activity. If she is incorrect, another child may take a turn. If she reaches home plate, she scores a run. Have her keep a cumulative total of the runs scored. At the end of the game, the child with the most runs wins.

Walt Disney

Walt Disney was an American cartoonist famous for his achievements in the field of entertainment. In 1928, one of Disney's characters, Mickey Mouse, appeared in the first cartoon with synchronized sound. Disney's other films include *Snow White And The Seven Dwarfs, Mary Poppins, Bambi,* and *Fantasia.* Disney won over one hundred awards for his films. He has two theme parks in the United States named after him: Disneyland in California and Walt Disney World in Florida.

Use the popularity of the Disney characters to focus on graphing. Draw a grid on a large sheet of paper or chalkboard. Attach pictures of five different Disney characters to the left of the grid (a Disney coloring book is a good source of pictures). Ask each child to attach a paper square beside her favorite character. Afterwards compare and discuss the results.

Henry Ford

Henry Ford did not build the first automobile. However, he made the automobile affordable and available to people from all walks of life, forever changing the way Americans lived and worked. Allow a small group of children to measure the distance a toy car will roll. Place a long sheet of paper on the floor. Let the children use blocks to build an inclined plane at one end of the paper as shown. Tell them to roll a toy car down the incline. Instruct them to make a mark on the paper behind the car to indicate where it stopped. Ask them to build a different inclined plane beside the first one and repeat the procedure with the same toy car. Have them compare the two distances marked on the paper to determine which is longer. To extend the activity, let the youngsters turn the paper over and repeat the process.

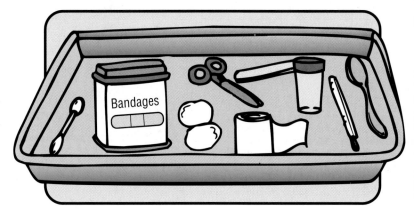

Clara Barton

Clara Barton was a nurse who cared for the sick and wounded during the Civil War. After the war, she founded the American Red Cross, an organization that helps people in times of disaster. Collect several objects a nurse might use such as a box of bandages, a cotton ball, a pair of scissors, a gauze strip, an empty bottle of medicine, a tissue, a thermometer, a tongue depressor, a spoon, and a cotton swab. Place the objects on a tray. Let a small group of children observe the objects for one minute. Then cover the tray with a towel. Ask the youngsters to name the objects without looking under the towel. List each one on a sheet of chart paper as it is named. Afterwards, uncover the tray and check the list to see how many were remembered. To vary the activity, tell the children to close their eyes, and take away one object after the children have observed the objects for a minute. Then ask them to open their eyes and name the object that is missing.

LANGUAGE ARTS

Thomas Edison

Thomas Edison was probably America's greatest inventor. Edison invented the phonograph and the electric lightbulb. He also made improvements on other inventions, such as the telephone, typewriter, and motion picture. Draw the outline of a lightbulb on the chalkboard. Write several alphabet letters inside the bulb. Point to one letter. Ask your children to call out as many words as they can that begin with the letter's sound. Then turn off the light by erasing the letter. Repeat the activity with each letter.

George Washington

What did George Washington like to eat for breakfast? Read aloud *George Washington's Breakfast* by Jean Fritz to find the answer to this question. Then have your youngsters make a class book titled "My Breakfast." Begin by asking each child what she likes to eat for the first meal of the day. Write the child's name and the sentence "I like to eat _____ for breakfast" on a sheet of chart paper. Next have each child copy her sentence on a sheet of paper (write the sentence for young children) and illustrate it. Then bind the papers inside a bright-colored cover.

Helen Keller

When Helen Keller was nineteen months old, she contracted a severe illness that left her deaf and blind. With the help of her teacher, Anne Sullivan, Keller learned to "hear" others speak by placing her fingers on their lips and throats when they spoke. Sullivan also taught Keller to read braille and to speak. In spite of her handicaps, Keller wrote several books and worked to help those who were also deaf and/or blind. After sharing this information with your children, show them an example of a braille book. Tell them that people who cannot see can read by running their fingers along the series of raised dots. Then show your youngsters how people who cannot hear or speak communicate. Teach your youngsters to sign a few alphabet letters or simple phrases such as "I love you." The book *Signing Made Easy: A Complete Program For Learning Sign Language* by Rod R. Butterworth and Mickey Flodin is a good reference.

An Wang

An Wang was a Chinese-American inventor and business executive. Wang invented a key component in the evolution of the modern computer. Give each child a copy of the computer keyboard on page 12. Call out each letter in random order. Ask children to "type" each letter on the keyboard. To vary the activity, ask your children to "type" basic sight words on their computer keyboards.

Dr. Seuss

Theodor Seuss Geisel, or Dr. Seuss as he was better known, wrote and illustrated books for children who were beginning to read. His books include *Green Eggs And Ham, How The Grinch Stole Christmas,* and *And To Think That I Saw It On Mulberry Street.* Read aloud *The Cat In The Hat* by Dr. Seuss. Afterwards ask your children to name words that rhyme with *hat.* List these words on a sheet of chart paper. Then give each child a copy of the pattern on page 13. Tell her to color the hat. Then have her cut out the hat and paper strip. Cut along the dotted lines and thread the strip through the two slits. Ask the child to read each of the rhyming words created as she gently pulls the strip through the slits.

The Wright Brothers

Orville and Wilbur Wright were inventors. They designed, built, and flew the first successful motor-driven airplane. Have each child pretend he is a famous inventor. Tell him to draw a picture of what he would invent. Next have him dictate a sentence describing the invention. Print the sentence on the picture. Then let him share his drawing with the class.

Julia Child

Julia Child is a food expert, an author, and a television star. When Child was first married, she knew little about cooking. However, during her six-year stay in France, she attended cooking school. Later she opened a restaurant in Paris and wrote a cookbook.

Assemble a small group of children around a table. Ask each child to pretend she is a world-famous chef. Give her a pretzel rod, a plastic knife, a small container of cream cheese, and a few raisins. Then ask her to follow your step-by-step directions for making Ants On A Log. After she has made the snack, let her eat it. Afterwards let the group describe how the snack was prepared. List each step on a sheet of chart paper. Then read the recipe aloud to the children as it was dictated.

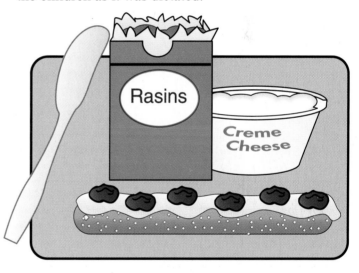

Maurice Sendak

Maurice Sendak is a world-renowned author-illustrator. His books include such children's favorites as *Where The Wild Things Are, In The Night Kitchen,* and *Outside Over There.* In 1970, Sendak received the Hans Christian Andersen Illustrator Award for the excellence of his entire body of work. Read aloud Sendak's book *Pierre: A Cautionary Tale in Five Chapters And A Prologue.* After discussing the story, reread it with the help of your youngsters. Write the sentence "I don't care!" on the chalkboard. Each time you come to the sentence in the story, point to it on the chalkboard and have your children read it together.

SCIENCE

George Washington Carver

George Washington Carver was a painter, musician, college professor, and plant scientist. Carver made hundreds of useful things—such as paper, shampoo, and ink—from peanuts. He made other products—such as soap, starch, and coffee—from sweet potatoes. To remind your children of Carver's accomplishments, root a sweet potato and watch the roots and leaves form. Select a sweet potato that is beginning to show a few roots. Then partially fill a glass jar with water. Place a small lump of charcoal in the water to keep the sweet potato from rotting. Set the potato in the neck of the jar so approximately one inch of the small end is in the water. Place the container in a sunny window and keep the water fresh.

Benjamin Franklin

Benjamin Franklin had many talents. He was a printer, a diplomat, an educator, a philosopher, a scientist, and an inventor. However, Benjamin Franklin is probably best known for his experiments with electricity. Show children how they can charge an object with static electricity. Cut a strip of tissue paper into thin streamers, leaving one end uncut. Rub a wool cloth over an inflated balloon. Hold the balloon near the tissue paper. The tissue-paper streamers will move toward the balloon.

Alexander Graham Bell

Alexander Graham Bell was a teacher of the deaf and the inventor of the electric telephone. To demonstrate how a vibration produces sound, have each child in a small group stretch a rubber band around a plastic drinking glass as shown. Tell him to place the bottom of the glass up to his ear and gently strum the rubber band across the top. The rubber band will vibrate, causing the air to move. The plastic glass will transmit the vibrations to the child's ear, producing a distinct sound.

Leonard Bernstein

Leonard Bernstein was a conductor, composer, and pianist. He conducted the world-famous New York Philharmonic Orchestra for eleven years, often performing as a solo pianist. Create an orchestra in your classroom and let each child take a turn being the conductor. Allow each of the other children to play one of the instruments described below. Then let your classroom orchestra play along with a recording of a favorite song.

Soda-Bottle Wind Instrument—Blow gently across the mouth of an empty soda bottle. To vary the sound, add water at different heights.

Comb Synthesizer—Wrap a strip of tissue paper around a clean comb two or three times. Hold the tissue paper in place with your hand. Place the comb up to your mouth and hum with parted lips.

Tin Can Drum—Strike the bottom of an empty tin can or pie tin with a pencil or wooden dowel.

SOCIAL STUDIES

Jimmy Carter

Many famous people work for others, not just for themselves. After leaving office, former President Jimmy Carter began working with the Habitat For Humanity organization building homes for people who could not afford to buy one. Share information with your children about Carter's work. Then have them think of ways they could help those less fortunate than themselves. Extend the helpfulness by asking each child to bring in a can of food to share with a local soup kitchen or a book for a children's hospital.

Dr. Martin Luther King, Jr.

Dr. Martin Luther King, Jr., was an African-American minister who worked for equal rights for all citizens. In his "I Have A Dream" speech, King expressed his desire for all Americans to live, work, and play together in harmony. Read aloud *Happy Birthday, Martin Luther King* by Jean Marzollo. Afterwards ask your children to discuss their hopes and dreams for the people of our country. For example, a student might say, "I wish people would not fight." List the ideas on a sheet of chart paper. Then have each child draw a picture to illustrate his dream on a cloud cutout. Attach the pictures to a bulletin board titled "I Have A Dream."

A Famous Visitor

Tell each child in a small group to imagine he were able to invite any famous American to spend one day with him. Ask him to name the person he would invite and tell why. Then ask him to describe what they would do together.

Local Heroes

Many towns and communities can boast of a local person who made a significant contribution to our American heritage. Monuments, buildings, streets, and parks are often named for these individuals. Tell your children about a famous American from your area or state. Then take the children on a field trip to visit the location named for the person.

ART

Eric Carle

Eric Carle is one of America's best-loved authors and illustrators. Carle creates the illustrations for his books by preparing his own colored tissue papers. He splashes, spatters, and fingerpaints acrylic paints onto the tissue papers to achieve a variety of textures. Then he cuts or tears the papers into shapes and glues them onto an illustration board. Let each child in a small group use a technique similar to Carle's to create a beautiful picture. Place different-colored fingerpaints, fingerpaint paper, paintbrushes, and several instruments for printing in a learning center. Tell each child to use her fingers, a paintbrush, or one of the printing instruments to cover a sheet of paper with paint. When the paint has dried, cut each sheet of paper to equally divide it among the children. Then ask each child to create a picture by cutting the different-colored papers into shapes and attaching them to a sheet of construction paper.

I. M. Pei

I. M. Pei *(pay)* is one of America's best architects. Pei designs buildings to be friendly to the people they serve. Pei has completed over 100 projects and has received over 100 awards for his work. In a small group, have each budding architect build a house, skyscraper, or tower from cards. To prepare for the activity, obtain a package of 3" x 5" index cards. Cut slits in each card as shown in the illustration. Tell each child to join the cards at the slits to create a unique structure.

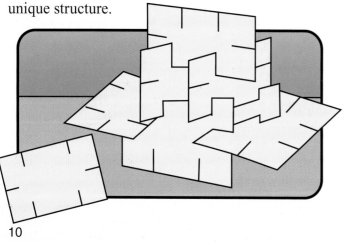

Betsy Ross

No one is certain who sewed the first official American flag. However, according to tradition, a seamstress named Betsy Ross made it. Her grandson first told the story of how General George Washington visited her shop. He asked Ross to make the flag based on his rough pencil sketch. Ross suggested a few changes, such as using a five-pointed star rather than a six-pointed one. Then she carried out the commission. Let each child in a small group try his hand at sewing. Have him use paints or markers to color a picture on a tagboard square or rectangle. Use a hole puncher to punch holes around the perimeter of the square. Wrap a piece of tape around one end to create a "needle" for sewing. Tell the child to pull the yarn in and out of the holes. Then tie the two ends together to secure the yarn.

Jim Henson

Jim Henson's Muppets have educated and entertained children for over thirty years. His television shows—"The Muppet Show," and "Sesame Street"—have been enjoyed by audiences around the world. Show each child in a small group how to make a simple hand puppet. Tell her to place her hand flat, with her fingers spread, on a folded piece of muslin. Trace around her hand with a fine-line marker to create a mitten shape. Cut around the outside of the folded outline, leaving a wide wrist. Use a sewing machine to stitch around the perimeter of the puppet, leaving the wrist open. Then let the child use fabric markers to draw a person or an animal on the front.

SNACK

For breakfast, George Washington ate three small Indian hoecakes and drank three cups of tea.

Hoecakes

Cut 1/2 cup of softened butter or margarine into 2 cups of self-rising flour. Blend the mixture with a fork until it resembles a coarse meal. Add enough buttermilk to make a soft dough. Knead for five minutes. Separate dough into two pieces. Place each piece into a greased baking pan or skillet. Pat down lightly. Brush with melted butter. Bake at 450° until golden brown. Serve with tea.

CULMINATING ACTIVITY

Famous Americans Day

Encourage each child to dress up as a famous American on the last day of the unit. Send home a note at the beginning of the week requesting that parents assist their child in choosing a famous American to represent. Have them then help their child locate the appropriate clothing and props to depict the famous American on the final day of the unit.

Computer Keyboard

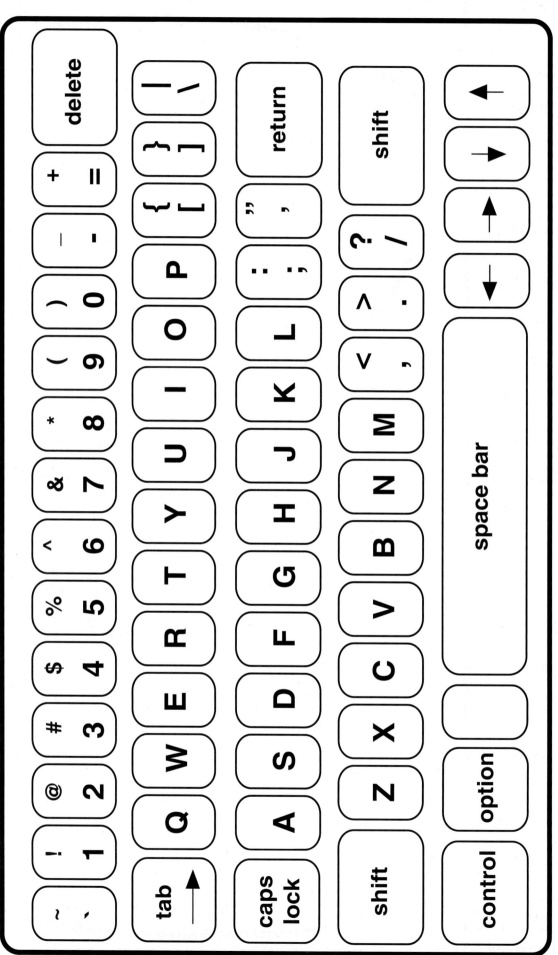

Pull

m s p f r

m h p b c

Pull

at

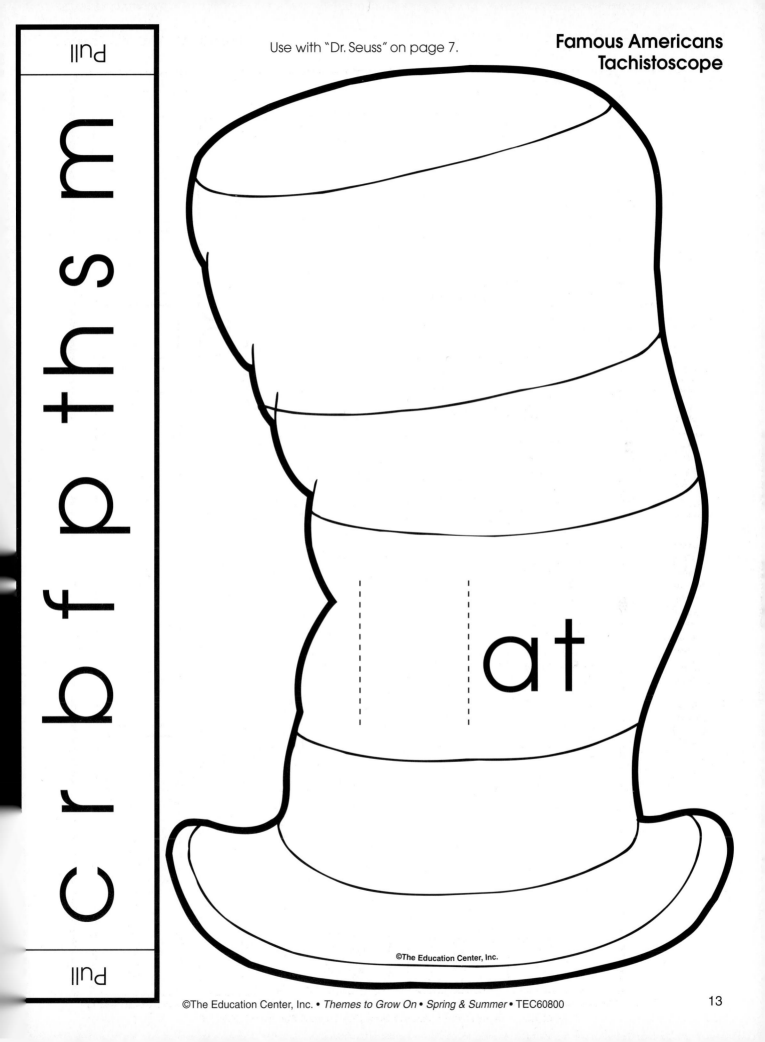

The Circus

Hurry, hurry, hurry! Step right up! Tightrope walkers, dancing clowns, jugglers, and acrobats—these are just a few of the circus performers who will provide thrills galore as you embark on this exciting trip under the big top.

MATH

Don't Feed The Elephants

Your children will want to play this game of strategy again and again. Divide the class into pairs. Give each pair thirteen packing peanuts. Ask the student pairs to place the peanuts in a line between them. Then tell them to take turns removing one, two, or three peanuts at a time from the line. The player who does not remove the last peanut wins.

Popcorn Estimation

Show your children a Styrofoam cup filled with un-popped popcorn kernels. Ask each child to estimate how many cups of popcorn one cup of kernels will make. Tell him to write his estimation on a slip of paper. Then pop the popcorn and pour it into Styrofoam cups. Count the cups. Compare each estimate with the actual number of cups.

Circus Acts

Have your children name five circus performers, such as the lion tamer, clown, tightrope walker, horseback rider, and acrobat. Draw a picture and write the name of each one on a graph. Ask each child to choose his favorite performer and put a circus sticker beside the appropriate picture and name. Compare the results when the graph is completed.

Circus Train

Make one copy of the engine pattern and ten copies of the train car pattern on page 22. Write a numeral from one to ten on each car. Glue the engine and train cars to a strip of tagboard. Laminate for durability. Place the circus train and a deck of number set cards in a learning center. Have the children place each card on the car with the corresponding numeral.

Peanuts

To prepare for this activity, fill a small container with peanuts in the shell (choose the ones that have two peanuts in the shell). Spread the peanuts out on a tabletop or counting mat visible to a small group. Tell students they can count the total number of peanuts without opening the shells. Ask the group to count the peanuts by twos. Then open the shells, remove the peanuts, and have them count by ones to check the total. (First check for peanut allergies among your class. Do not allow students to eat the peanuts.)

How Heavy?

Which is heavier—a tiger or an elephant? Give each child a copy of the reproducible on page 23. Tell him to cut out the pictures on the solid black lines. Then have him attach them to a strip of construction paper in order from the lightest item to the heaviest.

Circus Express

All aboard! Time to load up the circus train and travel to the next city. In which car will each of the animals ride? To prepare for the activity, use the reproducible on page 22 to make a circus train poster. Place the poster and a container of animal crackers in a learning center. Let the children work together to group the animal crackers on different cars. Then ask ordinal position questions such as "In which train car will the lions travel? The elephants?"

Popcorn Kernels

Show students a container of unpopped popcorn kernels, a container of popped popcorn, and a balance scale. Ask the children to help you use the scale to determine how much popped popcorn and popcorn kernels are needed to balance the scales.

LANGUAGE ARTS

Three-Ring Circus

Place three Hula-Hoops on the floor to represent the three rings in a circus. Place an assortment of objects in each one. Have your children sit in a large circle around the rings. Ask a student volunteer to select two objects from different rings and tell how they are alike (for example, you can juggle a beanbag and a ball). Return the objects to the rings. Repeat the activity until each child has had a turn.

Circus Talk

What is a *joey? Joey* is the circus word for "clown." Teach your youngsters the definitions of the circus words printed below. Then ask volunteers to use the words in sentences.

1. *hump*—a camel
2. *painted pony*—a zebra
3. *stripes*—a tiger
4. *butcher*—a person who sells food, drinks, or souvenirs to audience members
5. *bull*—a circus elephant
6. *big top*—a circus tent
7. *clown alley*—the clowns' dressing room
8. *kimber*—a circus performer
9. *razorbacks*—the people who set up the circus and take it down
10. *private person*—a person who is not with the circus

Elephant Parade

Print the poem "Holding Hands" by Lenore M. Link, from *The Random House Book Of Poetry For Children* selected by Jack Prelutsky, on a sheet of chart paper. Read the poem to your children. Then ask them to look for words in the poem that are repeated, such as *elephants, holding, hands,* and *tails.* Circle each set of matching words with a different-colored marker. Then reread the poem. Finally play "The Elephant" from the record *Learning Basic Skills Through Music* by Hap Palmer, and let your children pretend they are elephants in a circus parade.

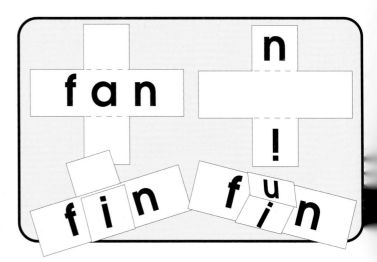

Tumbling Words

Your older children can make new words by changing the vowel in each of the tumbling words. Cut several word cards similar to the example above. Print one word in the center section of each individual card. Fold the top flap down and write a vowel on it. Fold the bottom flap up and write a different vowel on it. Place the word cards in a learning center. Ask each child in the center to choose a card and read the word in the center section. Then fold the flaps over one at a time and read the new words. Have him repeat the same procedure with the other word cards. Listed below are suggested sets of tumbling words.

tip	bet	net	fan
tap	but	nut	fin
top	bat	not	fun
pen	big	cat	
pan	bag	cot	
pin	bug	cut	

Popcorn

Cut several popcorn shapes from tagboard. Then cut beginning consonant pictures from an old phonics workbook. Glue each picture to a popcorn shape. Place them inside a popcorn box or bag. Ask the children in a small group to sort the pictures by beginning sounds. One note: Color code the back of each popcorn kernel to make the activity self-checking.

Ringmaster's Hat

Appearing in the center ring—a ringmaster's hat filled with words galore and one tricky rabbit! Print at least twenty-five sight words on individual cards. On one card draw or attach a picture of a rabbit. Place all the cards inside a top hat (if a top hat is not available, a simple one can be made from tagboard). Let each child, in a small group, take a turn drawing one card from the hat. If he can read the word, he may keep the card. If not, he returns it to the hat. If the rabbit card is drawn, all of the child's cards are returned to the hat. The game ends when one child collects five cards. To vary the activity for younger children, print alphabet letters on the cards.

Curious Sights

Each child will enjoy making a book titled "Circus Sights." Print several circus words, such as *clown, acrobat, tent, elephant,* and *tiger,* on individual cards. Draw or attach a picture of each word on the card. Place the word cards, paper, pencils, and crayons in a learning center. Have each child choose a card, copy the word on a sheet of paper, and illustrate it. Let her repeat the procedure as many times as she wants. Then bind the pages together inside a bright-colored cover.

Curious George

Read aloud *Curious George Rides A Bike* by H. A. Rey. Discuss the story; then give each child a sheet of paper folded into thirds. Have her draw a picture in each of the three sections: what happened at the beginning, middle, and end of the story. One note: Events shown in the pictures in the center section may vary.

SCIENCE

Circus Senses

The circus is filled with wonderful sights, sounds, tastes, and smells. Ask your children to pretend they are sitting under the big top watching the circus show. Have them describe what they see, hear, taste, and smell. Make a separate list for each sense. Then let each child make an individual book titled "At The Circus." On separate sheets of paper, print the sentences, "I see _____," "I hear _____," "I smell _____," and "I taste _____," one sentence per sheet. Tell each child to copy one word from each list in the appropriate blank and illustrate each sentence. Then bind the pages together.

Balloons

Show your youngsters how to inflate a balloon without blowing into it. Chill an empty glass jug in the refrigerator for one hour. Stretch the neck of a balloon over the jug opening. When the air inside the jug warms, it will expand and fill the balloon. Remove balloons from childrens' reach after finishing the demonstration.

Gross-Motor Games

Set up three stations in the classroom where your children can practice circus acts. Divide the class into small groups. Have the groups rotate through the stations until everyone has had a chance to practice each act.

Tightrope Walking—Borrow a balance beam from the Physical Education Department to use as a tight-rope. If a balance beam is unavailable, place a piece of lumber or a strip of masking tape on the floor. Tell each child to walk the length of the balance beam forward, backward, and sideways, balancing a beanbag on her head or holding a yardstick.

Stilt Walking—Use rope and large juice or coffee cans to make stilts (cover all sharp edges). Puncture two holes in opposite sides of each can near the top. Thread a five-foot piece of rope through the holes. Tie the ends of the rope together to be waist-high on each child. Have a child stand on a pair of cans and hold the ends of the rope. Let each child in the center practice walking on the stilts.

Balancing Act—Ask each child to balance a one-foot ruler vertically in the palm of his hand.

SOCIAL STUDIES

Circus Child

After reading about circus life, ask each child to pretend she is a circus performer. Have her describe her life as she completes the following sentences:

My home would be…
I would go to school at…
My parents would work at…
In my spare time, I would…
My friends would be…
I would play with…
My pets would be…

Clowns

Clowns are some of the most popular circus performers. Invite a professional clown to your classroom. Ask him to come dressed in his everyday clothes. Then have him show your class how he transforms himself into a clown with makeup and special clothing. If a clown is not available, ask a parent or fellow teacher to play the part. An excellent source of information is …*If You Lived With The Circus* by Ann McGovern.

Circus Families

Living in a circus is like having a great big family. Many of the circus performers are actually related. Children of the circus stars learn the family act from their parents. For homework, ask each child to think of a skill he has learned from a family member, such as painting, sewing, or gardening. Then set aside time during the week when he can demonstrate his handiwork for the others.

I Think I Can

Read *The Little Engine That Could* by Watty Piper. Discuss how the Little Blue Engine pulled the train filled with toys over the mountain to the boys and girls waiting below. Next set up an "I Can" center. Place several manipulatives on a table in the center and give each child a checklist similar to the one printed below. Ask him to try each manipulative and check off the ones he can work.

___ I can button a button.
___ I can cut out a circle.
___ I can zip a zipper.
___ I can work a puzzle.
___ I can tie a shoelace.

19

ART

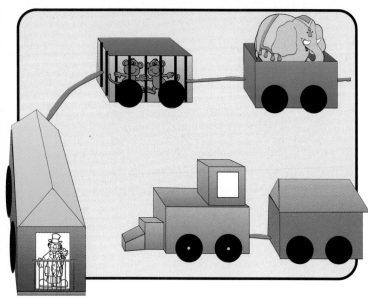

Cute Clown

Each child can create an attractive clown face using his imagination and these step-by-step directions. Sponge-paint an 18" x 24" sheet of paper for the background. Trace patterns for the head and collar on separate sheets of paper. Cut out the shapes. Sponge-paint the head using white tempera paint. When the paint is dry, attach the head and collar to the background paper. Decorate the collar with paint, sequins, stickers, or dyed macaroni. Next glue yarn to the head to create the hair. Then cut out a hat from wallpaper or wrapping paper, and attach it to the head. Use pasta to make the eyes, yarn or paper scraps for the mouth, and pasta for the nose.

Circus Train

This class circus train can be proudly displayed in the classroom, media center, or school showcase. To prepare for the project, collect an empty milk carton (half-gallon) for each child. Rinse the cartons, and let them dry. Cut off the top of each carton. Then have each child create a unique train car using the carton. Tell him to glue a strip of construction paper around the outside. Let him decorate the car with paint, markers, or paper scraps. Attach two black poster-board circles to each side for the wheels. Punch a hole in the front and back of each car. Connect the train cars by threading a piece of yarn through the holes. Create an engine for the train by gluing together boxes of various sizes and painting them black. Attach the engine to the cars. Place plastic circus animals in each car. Display the train in the classroom, media center, or school showcase.

Get Ready For The Big Day!

To prepare for Circus Day (see "Culminating Activity" on page 21), have your children make colorful posters, sponge-paint paper lunch bags for the popcorn, and create a ticket booth from a large cardboard box.

Popcorn Mosaic

Show your children how they can dye popcorn and use it to make an attractive mosaic. Fill several cups with water. Add different-colored food coloring to each one. Place a few kernels of popped corn into one cup. Stir once. Remove the popcorn quickly. Place the popcorn on a paper towel to dry completely. Repeat the procedure using the remaining colors and more popcorn. Next draw a simple design on a sheet of paper. Then spread glue on one area of the design and add the colored popcorn. Repeat in the same manner with the other areas. Let the mosaic dry overnight.

The Circus

SNACK

Ice-Cream Clown

Spoon thawed whipped cream onto a small plate. Sprinkle with colored sugar. Place a scoop of ice cream in the center of the whipped cream. Put a sugar cone on top of the ice cream. Push small candies such as M&M's into the ice cream to create the eyes, nose, and mouth.

CULMINATING ACTIVITY

Circus Day

On the last day of the unit, let your children perform in a classroom circus. Send a note home to parents explaining a designated activity or game so parents can help their children prepare. Allow your youngsters to wear costumes such as clown costumes and to make up or bring in props. On the day of the circus, give each child play money to buy tickets and popcorn. Then enjoy the show.

21

The Circus
Train patterns
Use with "Circus Train" on page 14 and "Circus Express" on page 15.

engine

train car

The Circus
Sequencing by weight
Use with "How Heavy?" on page 15.

The Wild West

Saddle up your horses for a rootin'-tootin' western adventure. The Wild West will come alive as your cowpokes square-dance, listen to tall tales, sing cowboy songs, and participate in rodeo activities.

MATH

Strike It Rich

Mining for gold was a popular occupation during the early settlement of the West. Have your "younguns" pretend to be miners while weighing and estimating the worth of gold nuggets. To create the gold nuggets for this activity, collect several small rocks and spray them with gold paint. Then use two different-sized metal bars or weights as the standards for weighing the nuggets. Spray-paint the bars gold. Label the smaller bar "five dollars" and the larger one "ten dollars." Then give each child in a small group a sack of gold nuggets. Let him determine how much his gold is worth by placing a gold bar on one side of a balance scale and enough nuggets to balance it on the other side. Then record the dollar amount of the set of nuggets on a sheet of paper. Have him repeat the procedure until all of the nuggets have been weighed. Then total the amount for each set to find the value of the bag of gold.

Roundup

Place a container of small plastic horses and cows in a center. Build several small fences using Popsicle ice pop sticks or Lincoln Logs toys on a table in the center. Have each child place a few horses and cows inside each of four or five fences. Then ask her to write a math equation on a paper strip to reflect the number of animals in each fence. For example, if there were six horses and four cows inside one fence, the child would write $6 + 4 = 10$.

Rope Tricks

In the days of the Wild West, a cowboy's hat served many purposes. He used it to shade his eyes from the sun, drink water from a stream, and cushion his head when he slept. Ask each child to bring a hat from home. Then use several large jump ropes to make circles on the classroom floor. Have the children think of a way to sort the hats in the circles. Then let each child place his hat inside the corresponding circle. Once the hats have been sorted, ask the children to think of another way to sort the hats and repeat the procedure.

Stick-In-The-Hoop

Have the children in a small group play a version of the Cheyenne game Stick-In-The-Hoop. Tie the ends of a three-foot rope together to form a hoop and place it on the floor. Then give each child in the group four sticks (sticks may be made by twisting small paper bags). Ask one child to walk two paces from the hoop, turn his back to it, and gently toss the sticks, one at a time, toward the hoop. Have him keep a tally of the number of sticks he gets in the hoop. Then let another child have a turn. Continue to play until one child reaches a predetermined number.

Western Puzzles

Collect ten pictures of various western scenes. Paste each picture on a piece of tagboard and laminate for durability. Then cut each picture apart to create three puzzle pieces. Place all the puzzle pieces in a box. Have the children in a small group re-create the pictures by placing the correct puzzle pieces together.

Calf Roping

Children will enjoy racing the clock as they perform these cowpoke stunts. Hang a bandana from a hook in the classroom. Designate this as the starting point for the calf-roping competition. Tell a child to walk to the bandana, tie it around his neck, and then proceed to another area in the room to pick up a rope. Have him carry the rope to another designated spot where there is a small chair with a picture of a cow face fastened to the back. Pretending the chair is a calf, have each student turn it over, wrap the rope around the four legs, and secure the ends. Use a stopwatch to time the activity from start to finish. Record the time on a sheet of chart paper. Put the bandana and the rope back in their respective places and set the chair upright again. Then let another child perform the activity. Compare the times of all the children to see who was the fastest.

Buckaroo Brands

Give each child a copy of the reproducible on page 32. Tell her to complete each of the brands by copying each brand shown in the space provided.

LANGUAGE ARTS

Going Out West

Children will test their memories and their initial consonant skills as they play Going Out West. Sit in a circle with six to ten children. Begin the game by saying, "I'm going out West and I'm taking _____." Complete the sentence with a word that begins with *A*. Have the child sitting to your left repeat the *A* word and then add a word that begins with a *B*. For example, "I'm going out West and I'm taking an apple and a bandana." The pattern continues until each child in the group has had a turn.

Storytellers

Invite a different storyteller to your room each day to tell your children a western tall tale. The storytellers may be parents, fellow teachers, or older children. Encourage your guests to dress up like cowboys and use props to tell their stories.

Cowboy Dress-Up

A cowboy's outfit was determined by need and not by looks. Collect some or all of the items listed below. Then have a student volunteer model each item for the class as you discuss its importance to the cowboy.

Hat— shielded eyes from the sun
used to drink water from a creek or river
used as a pillow

Bandana— kept dust out of eyes
used to blindfold a horse so it would not get spooked

Boots— the high heels kept feet in the stirrups
the high sides kept dirt off of feet and helped protect legs against snakebites

Spurs— used to urge a horse forward
Chaps— protected legs
Rope— used to lasso stray cows

The Wild West

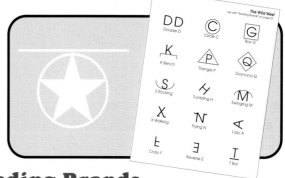

Circle R Ranch

Help your children increase vocabulary and practice word-recognition skills with the following activity. Draw a ranch site on a large sheet of paper. Include a ranch house, bunkhouse, corral, stable, horse, saddle, rope, dinner bell, field, water trough, and cowboys. Laminate the picture and attach it to a bulletin board. Then ask a student volunteer to name one of the objects in the picture. Write the picture's name on a word card, sounding out the word(s) as you write it (them). Then attach the word card to the picture with a thumbtack or tape. Continue the process until each part of the ranch has been identified. Take the word cards off the ranch scene. Then ask the children in a small group to reattach each card to the corresponding object in the picture. Repeat the activity with another small group of children.

Reading Brands

During the early days of the westward movement, there were no fences for cattle. Cowboys had to brand their cows with special markings in order to identify them. To read the cattle brands, cowboys followed three simple rules. Brands are read

1. from left to right
2. from top to bottom
3. from outside to inside

Discuss these rules with your children. Then give each child a copy of the reproducible on page 33. Read the brands to your youngsters. Then draw more complicated brands on the chalkboard. Ask for student volunteers to read the brands. Then let each child make up a brand of his own. Post the brands on a bulletin board titled "What's My Brand?"

Western Wear

Place a prop box filled with cowboy clothing and accessories in a learning center. Suggested items are a cowboy hat, a vest, a sheriff's badge, a rope, a frying pan, cooking utensils, a bandana, and a stick horse. Let the children in the center use the props to act out some of their favorite tall tales.

SCIENCE

Cactus Terrarium

Let your children work together to create a class terrarium. Cover the bottom of a clean aquarium with approximately three inches of sand. Plant several varieties of cacti in the sand. Add pretty rocks. Then sprinkle water into the terrarium to wet the sand. Finally place a vented cover over the top. Add more water when moisture beads are not seen on the inside of the glass.

Make A Tornado

Stories of the Wild West often contain tales of whirlwinds and tornadoes. Create a tornado in your classroom for your youngsters to observe. You will need two empty, plastic, two-liter soda bottles and a special device called a *tornado tube.* The device is inexpensive and may be purchased in many specialty toy stores. Fill one bottle two-thirds full with water. Screw the tornado tube onto the bottle's neck. Attach the second bottle to the first by screwing it to the other end of the tornado tube. Rotate the bottles so the full one is on top. Then move the upper bottle in a circular motion. Tornado action will occur. One note: special effects may be created by adding glitter and food coloring to the water.

Deserts

Discuss desert locations, landscapes, temperatures, annual rainfall, wildlife, and plant life. *A New True Book: Deserts* by Elsa Z. Posell and *Deserts* by Seymour Simon are excellent sources for information and pictures.

SOCIAL STUDIES

Pony Express

Pony express riders transported the mail in the days of the westward movement. These brave men traveled many treacherous miles to deliver letters to settlers eager to hear from families and friends. Let your youngsters pretend they are pony express riders as they participate in a relay. Divide the class into teams. Set up stations for exchanging riders. Then give the first member of each team a tote bag filled with junk mail. At a signal, have the children ride stick horses to awaiting team members and hand off the mail. The first team to complete the ride is the winner.

Barter Store

To barter is to exchange one article for another without the use of money. In the early settlement of the West, cowboys and miners would barter for items they needed when money was not available. Set up a barter store or trading post in your classroom. Then send a note home with each child requesting that she bring in two small, inexpensive items for use in the store. Tell your students one of the items will be used to stock the store and the other will be used to trade. Then set aside time for each child to visit the store to barter with her classmates.

Panning For Gold

Set up a learning center in your classroom where children can pan for gold. Add the gold nuggets used in the "Strike It Rich" activity on page 24 and rocks to a sand table or large container of sand. Mix the rocks and nuggets into the sand so they are not easily seen by your children. Then supply each young miner with a sand sifter or aluminum pie pan with holes punched in the bottom. Let her scoop up the sand with the sifter and sift through sand and the rocks to discover the gold.

Horses

Read aloud a factual book about horses, such as *A New True Book: Horses* by Elsa Z. Posell. Then ask your children to describe the various ways horses are used by people. List each item on a sheet of chart paper as it is dictated. Then invite a member of the mounted police, a riding instructor, or a horse owner to your class to talk about the care and training of horses.

Barter Store

ART

Sand-Cast Sculpture

Fill a large plastic tub with wet sand. Pack down the sand. Then scoop out an attractive design in the center. Place small twigs, shells, and stones in the hollowed-out sand. Pour plaster of paris into the hole. Insert a bent paper clip into the wet plaster to create a hook for the sculpture. Let it dry one hour. Then turn the tub of sand upside down and remove the plastic tub. Brush away the sand and let the sculpture dry completely.

Bucking Bronco

Every good cowboy or cowgirl needs a good horse, and your children are no exception. Ask each child to bring in a large, clean sock with a heel. Stuff the sock with batting, cloth, or strips of newspaper. Fasten the sock securely to the end of a stick with rubber bands (yardsticks work well and can be donated by a company or sent from home). Use a needle and thread, or glue, to attach buttons to the stuffed sock for the horse's eyes and yarn for its mane.

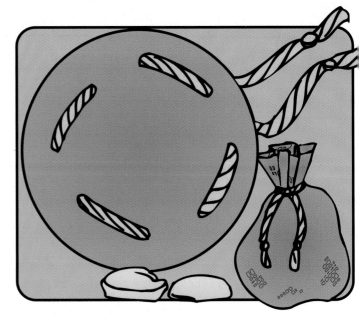

Gold Nugget Pouch

Let each child make a pouch for carrying gold nuggets. To prepare for the activity, cut a piece of burlap into a large circle for each child in a small group. Then use a pencil or piece of chalk to make a row of dots around the perimeter of the circle as a guide for sewing. The dots should be approximately one inch from the edge of the circle and 1 1/2 inches apart. Hole-punch each dot. Next give each child a length of yarn with one end taped like a shoelace. Let him push the thread through the right side of the fabric and pull it through the underside. Have him continue this procedure around the perimeter of the circle. Then tie a knot in both ends of the yarn. Pull the ends of the yarn to gather the fabric and create a pouch. Give each child a few rocks that have been spray-painted gold to put into his pouch.

Bandana

Use pinking shears to cut out a 20" x 20" piece of solid-colored fabric for each child. Supply each of your students with stencils, natural sponges, and fabric paint to decorate the fabric square. Have her place a stencil on the fabric, dip a sponge in the paint, and gently dab the paint in the center of the stencil. Repeat the process until the fabric square is covered. One note: stencils may be made by using an X-acto knife to cut designs in the centers of plastic lids.

SNACK

Trail Mix

Mix together equal amounts of Honey Nut Cheerios cereal, raisins, M&M's candies, and Corn Chex cereal. Serve in small plastic cups.

CULMINATING ACTIVITY

Let's Have A Rodeo

What better way to conclude this week's study of the Wild West than by having a rodeo? Encourage your students to come dressed as cowboys and cowgirls on Rodeo Day. Then plan several rodeo activities, such as those suggested below.

Square Dancing: Help your children enhance their gross-motor skills while dancing to traditional folk tunes. The *Wee Sing Fun 'N' Folk* CD and song booklet by Pamela Conn Beall and Susan Hagen Nipp include music and suggestions for movements for "Pawpaw Patch," "Buffalo Gals," "Turkey In The Straw," "Shoo Fly," and several others.

Barrel-Ride Relay: Divide the class into two teams. Place a row of four chairs in front of each team. Ask the first child in each team to ride a stick horse in a zigzag pattern through the line of chairs and then back. Have him tag the next child in line. The first team to complete the relay is the winner.

The Wild West

Use with "Buckaroo Brands" on page 25.

Look at each brand.
Trace.
Draw each brand.

©The Education Center, Inc. • *Themes to Grow On* • *Spring & Summer* • TEC60800

Double D

Circle C

Box G

K Bench

Triangle P

Diamond Q

S Rocking

Tumbling H

Swinging M

X Walking

Flying N

Lazy A

Crazy F

Reverse E

T Bar

Five Senses

Children will develop a heightened appreciation of the world around them as they see, hear, smell, touch, and taste their way through these "sense-sational" activities.

MATH

Counting (Hearing)

Have the children sit in a circle and count off by ones, twos, fives, and/or tens. Each child must listen carefully as the others count to know his number.

Counting Sounds
(Hearing, Sight)

Ring a bell or clap your hands several times. Have the children listen for the number of sounds. Have them hold up their fingers to show how many times they heard the sound. Vary the activity by making two sets of sounds. Make one set of sounds, wait, and then make the second set. Have the children write addition equations that represent the total number of sounds in both sets.

Rhythm Patterns (Hearing)

Read aloud *Chicka Chicka Boom Boom* by Bill Martin Jr. and John Archambault to a small group of children. Give each child a musical instrument (maracas and/or drums). Have the children use the instruments to explore various musical patterns. Read the story again and have the children play the same musical pattern each time they hear the refrain "Chicka Chicka Boom Boom." Extend the activity by adding musical instruments or changing them. Then have the children make up musical patterns for songs such as "Mary Had A Little Lamb," "London Bridge Is Falling Down," or "B-I-N-G-O."

"Feely" Sock (Touch)

This made-in-a-minute Feely Sock is a great way for each youngster to explore her sense of touch. For each Feely Sock that you'd like to make, place several items of interesting texture or shape in a large plastic cup. Beginning at the bottom of the cup, slip an adult tube sock over the cup until the bottom of the cup is in the toe of the sock. To use the Feely Sock, a child slips her hand through the sock opening and feels the items in the cup. Add lots of variety to this activity by asking youngsters to describe what they feel, guess what they are touching, or retrieve a specific item without using their eyes.

Estimation (Sight)

Place several small objects such as dried beans or candy in a glass jar. Have each child estimate the number of objects she sees in the jar. Record each child's estimate. Count the objects in the jar to determine which child came the closest to the correct number.

Classifying (Touch)

Divide four large sheets of construction paper in half using a marker. Label each of the four sheets as shown with one of the following pairs of labels:

> Hard/Soft
> Rough/Smooth
> Large/Small
> Heavy/Light

Place objects representing each of the eight categories in four separate shoeboxes. Label the boxes.

Hard And Soft Box—rock, cotton ball, penny, yarn, block

Rough And Smooth Box—sandpaper, stone, burlap, silk scarf

Large And Small Box—paper clip, peg, block, ball, eraser

Heavy And Light Box—tissue paper, magnet, weight, feather

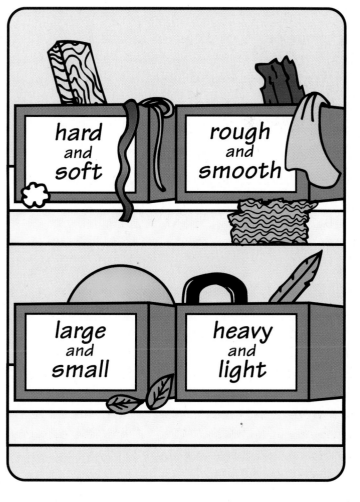

LANGUAGE ARTS

I Spy (Sight)

Put a twist on the traditional game of I Spy. Divide the class into four groups. Have a group of children look at one of the walls in the classroom. After a given amount of time, have the group members face away from the wall and name each of the objects they remember seeing. Repeat the process with the other groups. To vary the activity for a small group, have the children look at a detailed picture for a certain amount of time. Place the picture facedown and have the children name all of the things they remember seeing.

Listening To Letter Sounds (Hearing)

Have the children in a small group listen carefully as you say a pair of words. Have the children tell if the words sound the same at the beginning, in the middle, or at the end of each word.

> sheep—shoe *(beginning)*
> dog—pig *(end)*
> hat—can *(middle)*

A Sensory Language Experience (All Senses)

Each child can make a "Five Senses" book he can read on his own. Select a different sense to write about each day of the unit. Give each child a sheet of paper with one of the following incomplete sentences printed at the bottom:

> I can see a _____.
> I can smell a _____.
> I can hear a _____.
> I can taste a _____.
> I can touch a _____.

Have each child dictate the word or words he wants written in the blank to complete the sentence. Older children may write the completion on their own. Have each child illustrate his sentence. At the end of the week, bind the pages together to make individual sensory books.

Story Sounds (Hearing)

Before reading aloud a familiar book to the children, assign specific sounds to certain characters or actions in the story. Have the children make the sounds at the appropriate points in the story.

Senses Signals (All Senses)

Read a familiar story, like *Goldilocks And The Three Bears,* to the children. Have the children make the following signals each time one of the following words are read:

See or Saw—Make glasses with fingers around eyes.

Taste or Tasted—Stick out tongues.

Feel or Felt—Wiggle fingers.

Hear or Heard—Wiggle ears.

Smell or Smelled—Sniff noses.

Sound Toss (All Senses)

Label each of five shoeboxes with the name of one of the five senses. Place a few small plastic letters in each box. Put the boxes and a beanbag in a learning center. Have the children in the center take turns tossing the beanbag into a box. Have the child choose a letter from the box, say the sound it makes, and name something that begins with that sound and is associated with the sense. If a child chooses a *T* from the hearing box, he may say *trumpet.* If a child chooses *S* from the taste box, he may say *sandwich.*

Language Experience (Hearing)

Read *The Wheels On The Bus* adapted by Paul O. Zelinsky. Discuss the various sounds mentioned in the book. Have the children make a class book using the same format. The title might be "The Children In The Class." Sentences may be similar to the following:

"The clock on the wall goes tick, tick, tick, tick, tick, tick, tick, tick, tick. The clock on the wall goes tick, tick, tick all the school day long."

"The water in the sink goes drip, drip, drip, drip, drip, drip, drip, drip, drip. The water in the sink goes drip, drip, drip all the school day long."

Have the children work in pairs to write and illustrate one original sentence. Bind the pages together to create a class book.

SCIENCE

Sight Box

Make a sight box to help the children understand that light is needed to help us see. Cover a shoebox with a secure-fitting lid. Use a pencil to punch a small hole in one end of the box. Cut out a two-inch-square opening from the center of the lid. Use a brad to attach a heavy piece of black paper to the lid so that it covers the opening and keeps out the light. Remove the lid and tape a small object to the bottom of the box directly beneath the opening.

Have the children experiment with the sight box in a small group. Cover the opening in the lid with the flap and have each child look through the hole. Then open the flap and have each child take another peek through the hole. Discuss with the children why they can see the object when the flap is open and cannot see it when the flap is closed.

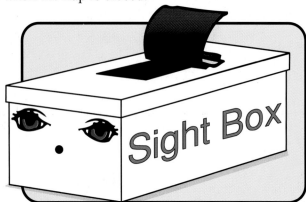

The Nose Knows

Make several smelly jars for this experiment. To make smelly jars, collect the following supplies: ten baby food jars, ten pieces of gauze, ten smelly foods (peanut butter, an onion, coffee, a lemon, vanilla extract, cinnamon, chewing gum, peppermint extract, vinegar, an orange), and pictures of each food. Wrap each food item in a piece of gauze and place it in a baby food jar. Color code the jars and corresponding pictures for easy checking. Have the children in a learning center open the jars one at a time and smell the contents. Then have the children match the pictures to the jars. Baby food jars may be spray painted to make them opaque.

Name That Tune

Children will enjoy experimenting with sound as they play Name That Tune. To conduct the experiment, use three identical glasses or glass jars, a metal spoon, water, and food coloring. Strike the empty glasses with the metal spoon. Have the children listen carefully to the sound. Pour water into each glass at a different level. Strike the glasses again and have the children listen carefully to the sounds. Add water to or pour out water from each jar to make the tones match the first three notes of the scale. Arrange the glasses by sound from lowest to highest. Place a few drops of red food coloring in the first jar, blue in the second jar, and green in the last jar. Have a child strike the jars with the spoon as you call out the following colors, or prepare a poster with the colors arranged in the correct order. Ask the children to name that tune once it has been played.

"Mary Had A Little Lamb"
green, blue, red, blue, green, green, green,
blue, blue, blue,
green, green, green.
green, blue, red, blue, green, green, green.
green, blue, blue, green, blue, red.

Extend the activity by adding jars dyed with other colors. Have the children play other familiar tunes or make up some of their own.

Tasting Party

Have a tasting party so the children can experiment with the sense of taste. Give each child a small plate with the following food items: pretzels (salty), marshmallows (sweet), dill pickle chip (sour), and unsweetened chocolate (bitter). Have the children taste each item, one at a time, and describe how it tastes. Give each child a copy of the lab sheet on page 42. Have him draw a picture of each of the foods he has tasted in the corresponding box.

Touch And Tell

Place a variety of objects in a "feely" sock (see "'Feely' Sock" on page 35). Have each child in a small group reach in the cup and feel one of the objects. Have him name three characteristics (such as *hard, smooth, slick, bumpy,* and *heavy)* of the object. Then ask him what he thinks the object is before he pulls it out of the cup. Continue the activity until everyone in the group has had a turn.

What's The Sense? Cut-And-Paste

After each of the five senses has been discussed, have the children complete the cut-and-paste worksheet on page 43.

SOCIAL STUDIES

Voice Identification (Hearing)

Tape the voice of each child in the classroom. Play the tape and have the children identify who is talking.

Community Workers (All Senses)

Invite a pediatrician to visit your classroom. Ask her to talk about how she examines a child's eyes, ears, nose, and mouth. She may also discuss how to care for each of these important parts of the body. If a pediatrician is not available, a specialist or a therapist will also provide the children with important information.

Following Rules (Sight, Hearing, Touch, Smell)

People need rules to live together and keep our world safe. Our senses help us be aware of these rules and warn us of danger. Discuss with the children how we use our senses to obey rules. For example, our eyes help us read rules such as traffic signs and warning labels. Our ears help us hear school fire alarms, car horns, and sirens. Our noses help warn us of potential dangers such as smoke and chemicals. After the discussion, have the children draw or cut out pictures from magazines of people using one of their senses to help them follow rules.

ART

Texture Collage (Touch)

Have each child bring in at least one or up to five items of various textures (cotton balls, burlap, ribbon, sandpaper). Attach the items to a piece of poster board and place it in a learning center for the children to touch. Vary the activity by having the children classify the items by texture before attaching them to the poster board. If you do this variation, attach the items by classification to the poster board.

Rhythm Band Instruments (Sound)

Have each child make one of the rhythm band instruments featured, or let her invent an instrument of her own. Let the children use their completed instruments in a parade around the classroom or the school.

Kazoo—Paint a paper-towel tube. Stretch waxed paper over one end and secure it with a rubber band. Play by humming in the open end.

Rattle—Decorate a plastic bottle by applying tissue paper to the outside with liquid starch. Pour a handful of dried beans in the bottle, replace the lid, and shake it to play.

Tambourine—Use a hot glue gun to glue the rims of two plastic plates together. Use a hole puncher to punch holes around the rim approximately one inch apart. Have the child lace a piece of yarn through each hole, adding a small bell in six places. Shake the tambourine to play.

Rubber Band Instrument—Remove the lid from an empty shoebox. Cover the shoebox with aluminum foil. Stretch rubber bands of different widths and thicknesses around the center of the box. Play by gently strumming the rubber bands.

Shaker—Paint a toilet-paper roll. When it is dry, punch four holes around both ends of the roll. Use yarn or heavy string to tie small bells in each of the holes. Shake it to play.

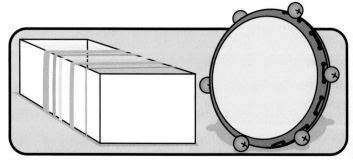

SNACK

Peanut Butter Play Dough
(Touch, Smell, Taste)

peanut butter (or soy nut butter)
nonfat dry milk

Mix equal parts of peanut butter and nonfat dry milk together until the dough is the consistency of play dough. Add more peanut butter or dry milk as needed. Encourage the children to feel, smell, and taste the play dough as they use it to make various creations. (Caution: Please check for children with peanut allergies before using this activity.)

CULMINATING ACTIVITY

Five Senses Scavenger Hunt

Have your youngsters take a five senses scavenger hunt in your classroom. To prepare for a scavenger hunt, bring in 10 to 15 different items that easily lend themselves to the Five Senses unit. Write the name and a brief description of each item on a separate index card. Then show your students each of the items and discuss the various sensory characteristics of each one. Randomly place the items around your classroom. Then read aloud the description of each item from the index card. Have pairs of children try to locate the item that is being described. Below are some suggested items and descriptions for the scavenger hunt. Happy hunting!

- something that tastes sour (lemon)
- something that is rough to touch (sandpaper)
- something that is pleasant to smell (flower)
- something that tastes sweet (honey)
- something that makes a loud sound (horn)
- something that makes a ticking sound (a clock)
- something that feels soft (cotton)
- something that looks colorful (a picture of a rainbow)
- something that smells spicy (cloves or cinnamon)
- something to look through or read (a book)

"Sense-sational" Science

Salty

Bitter

Sweet

Sour

Use with "Tasting Party" on page 38.

Name _____

What's The Sense?

©The Education Center, Inc. • *Themes to Grow On* • *Spring & Summer* • TEC60800

Use with "What's the Sense? Cut-And-Paste" on page 39.

43

Energy

Your children will explore, discover, experiment, and exercise creative-thinking skills as they begin to understand energy and how it is used in their world.

MATH

Sun Power

Lay two thermometers side by side in a sunny place. Check and record the temperature on each one. Then cover one thermometer with a sheet of black construction paper and the other with a sheet of white construction paper. Wait thirty minutes and remove both sheets of paper. Read and record the temperature on each thermometer. Then ask your youngsters the following questions:

- Which thermometer showed the highest temperature? Why?
- Which color absorbed more heat?
- Which color would you wear on a sunny day if you wanted to stay cool?

Repeat the experiment with other colors of construction paper. Use contrasting shades of light and dark paper each time.

Boat Race

For homework, ask each child to design and make a sailboat. The next day have student pairs race their boats in a water table, large tub, or small swimming pool. Have them move their boats by blowing on them. Then have the winners race each other to determine a class champion.

Energy In Homes

For homework have each child find out how her home is heated. Then make a class graph programmed with natural gas, wood, oil, solar, electric, and combinations of heat sources. On the following day, have each child place an *X* under the heading that tells how her home is heated. Compare and contrast the information on the graph.

Our Home Energy Sources	
Gas	X X X X X X X X
Wood	X X
Oil	X X X X X
Solar	X X X X
Electric	X X X X X X X X
Combinations	X X X X X

How Many Clips?

Energize your youngsters when using magnets in your classroom. Display a container of paper clips and several magnets of different sizes, shapes, and strengths in a center. Tell each child in a small group to predict how many paper clips each of the magnets will attract. Have him write his predictions on a lab sheet. Then help him use the magnets to pick up the paper clips. Have each child write the actual number of paper clips picked up by each magnet on the lab sheet. Ask him to compare each prediction with the actual number of paper clips picked up by the magnet.

Air Power

Fire needs oxygen to burn. Place several balls of clay in a line on a large piece of cardboard. Insert a birthday candle in each one. Place a different-sized jar behind each of the candles. Tell your youngsters you will light the candles and then place the jars over them. Ask your children to predict which candle will burn the longest. Graph the predictions by having each child place a block beside the jar of his choice. Perform the experiment. Then determine which predictions were correct and why. To vary the activity, place different-sized candles under jars of equal size and shape, and repeat the procedure.

Cover The Sun

Make one copy of the sun reproducible and several copies of the cloud reproducible on page 52 for each child in a small group. Have each child cut out his patterns. Tell him to place the sun cutout on the floor and stand two feet away from it, facing the cutout. Tell him to toss the clouds at the sun until it is completely covered. Have him count the total number of clouds on the floor. Ask the children to compare their numbers. The child with the least number of clouds tossed to cover the sun is the winner. Hint: The clouds should be made from a sturdy paper such as tagboard.

LANGUAGE ARTS

The Farmer's Hat

The wind is a natural source of energy. In the story *Who Took The Farmer's Hat?* by Joan L. Nŏdset, the energy of the wind takes the farmer's hat on a journey. Along the way, the hat takes on the appearance of various objects as seen through the eyes of different animals. Read the book aloud to your class. Then have your youngsters name in sequence the different ways the hat was used in the story. Have six student volunteers dramatize the sequence of events using a straw hat. Let each child pretend to be one of the animals. Tell him to hold the hat, describe how it was used by the animal, and pass it to the next child. Continue until all six children have had a turn. Then repeat the activity with another group of children.

Finally let each child make a flip book of the story. Fold three sheets of paper as pictured above. Staple the papers together at the top. Then let the child use colored pencils to illustrate the various uses of the hat on the six pages of the book.

Sun Words

Make a copy of the reproducible on page 53 on yellow construction paper for each child. Have him cut out the picture of the sun and the letter strip. Cut on each sun's dotted lines with an X-acto knife. Help each child insert his strip through the slits as shown. Then pull the strip through and program it with letters that would make words that end in *un*.

Power Poetry

Help the children in a small group write simple, descriptive poems about the sun, wind, and water (see the examples below).

sun	wind	water
hot, bright	gentle, moving	wet, cold
sun	wind	water

Print the poems on chart paper as they are dictated by the children. Then let each child copy each poem on an individual sheet of paper. Bind the papers inside a bright-colored cover to create a book.

The sun is hot and bright. It gives us light.

The wind is slow and fast, and lasts and lasts.

water wet and cold water

Magnetic Letters

Place magnetic letters of the alphabet in random order on a magnetic board. Then play a song on a cassette recorder and have a child try to put the letters in order before the song ends.

Class Book

Place a variety of objects in a paper bag. Make sure there is one object for each child in the classroom. Let each child take one object from the bag. Have her predict whether a magnet will attract the object. Ask her to draw a picture of the object on a sheet of paper. If the object is attracted by a magnet, have her write, "A magnet will attract [the object]." If the object is not attracted by a magnet, have her write, "A magnet will not attract [the object]." Bind the pages together to create a class book.

Energy Fable

Read "The North Wind And The Sun" from *Aesop's Fables* selected and edited by Laura Harris. Ask your children to tell why the sun could make the man remove his coat and the wind could not. Then have three volunteers act out the story using a winter coat.

I Spy

Label a small bulletin board "I Spy Energy." Then, each day of the week, ask small groups of children to bring in energy pictures from home. Let each child describe how energy is being used in the picture. Then attach the picture to the bulletin board.

Energy Words

Print several energy words or high-frequency words on individual strips of tagboard. Laminate them for durability. Then attach a piece of magnetic tape to the back of each strip. Have each child in a small group select a word and place it on a magnetic board. Then let her spell the word on the board using magnetic letters.

SCIENCE

Sun Tea

Fill a gallon jar with water. Place three large tea bags in the water. Secure the lid on the jar. Set the jar in the sun until the water turns a golden shade of brown. Remove the tea bags and add sugar to sweeten the tea. Serve it over ice.

Water Wheel

Purchase a package of six-inch paper plates. Draw six lines on each plate as shown in the example below. Use a pair of scissors to poke a hole in the center of each plate. Then give a plate to each child in a small group. Tell him to cut on the lines to create six sections. Have him fold each section as shown to make a flap. Insert a plastic drinking straw through the hole. Then, with the flaps pointing up, hold the water wheel under running water and watch it turn.

Wind Power

On a windy day, wet several cloth and paper objects, such as a sock, washcloth, handkerchief, paper towel, cotton T-shirt, and cloth diaper. Hang them outside to dry in the wind. Then ask your children to predict the order in which the objects will dry. Check the objects at different times during the day to determine whether the predictions were correct. Finally ask your youngsters to discuss why some objects dried faster than others.

Magnetic Attraction

Place several small objects—such as a rubber band, paper clips, an eraser, a spring, a staple, a coin, a shell, a golf tee, and a safety pin on a tray. Supervise a child as he uses a magnet to see which objects it will pick up and which it will not. Then have him draw a picture of each object attracted by the magnet on a lab sheet.

Push Or Pull

Do you push or pull a tube of toothpaste? How about a wheelbarrow? Assemble various objects such as a wagon, a toy vacuum cleaner, a bottle of glue, and a pull toy in a learning center. Ask the children in the center to predict how to move each of the objects. Have each child record his predictions on a lab sheet like the one shown. Then move the objects and make checks beside the predictions which were correct. Be sure to point out that some objects can be both pushed *and* pulled, so either answer can be correct.

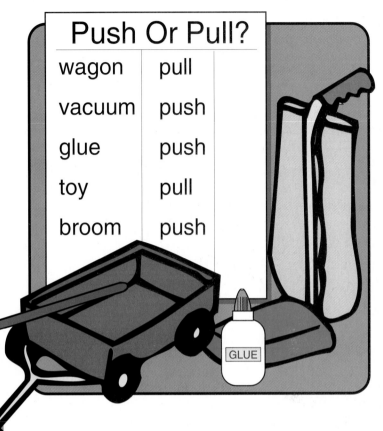

Push Or Pull?	
wagon	pull
vacuum	push
glue	push
toy	pull
broom	push

SOCIAL STUDIES

Community Worker

Invite an electrician, a power company representative, or a heating and cooling specialist to talk to your youngsters. Ask the person to discuss his or her work with energy. Also ask the presenter to bring some related tools for the children to handle and observe.

Energy Search

Help each child discover some of the ways energy is used in his home. Duplicate a checklist with questions similar to those listed below. Then for homework, have each child answer the questions with the assistance of a parent.

1. Is there a windsock or flag at your home? Yes   No
2. Do you have magnets on the front of your refrigerator? Yes   No
3. Are there wind chimes outside your home? Yes   No
4. Do you have a solar calculator?   Yes   No
5. Do you have an electric can opener with a magnet that holds a lid once it is removed from a can? Yes   No
6. Is there a room with many windows in your home that becomes warm on a sunny day? Yes   No

ART

Solargraphics®

In the past, *sun pictures* were made by placing objects on sheets of dark paper and leaving them in the sun for several days. With Solargraphics paper, the same activity can be done in a matter of minutes. Solargraphics paper is inexpensive and can be purchased at a nature store or science museum gift store. The directions for its use are printed on each packet of paper.

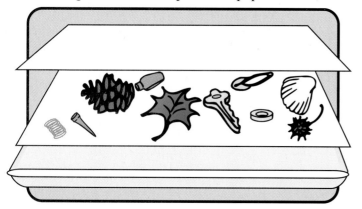

Wind Wheel

Your children will enjoy making attractive wind wheels that demonstrate the power of moving air. To create a wind wheel, each child will need tape, a paper plate, a pencil, a thumbtack, markers, and four small paper cups. Decorate the plate and cups using markers. Then tape the cups around the perimeter of the plate as shown. Attach the center of the plate to the eraser end of the pencil with the thumbtack, making sure the plate turns easily. Turn the wind wheel by blowing into the cups or taking it outside on a windy day.

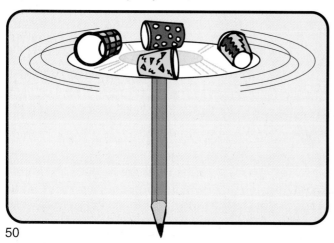

Fish Windsock

Give each child a large sheet of finger-paint paper or paper of similar weight. Then demonstrate how to fold over approximately two inches of one of the shorter ends, and let each child do the same. Next draw a picture of a fish on your paper and instruct the children to follow your example, not copy it. When the children's drawings are complete, let them cut fringe along the end opposite the folded end. Next have each child glue the two long ends of his paper together, let it dry, and then use a hole puncher to make two holes in the folded end of the paper. Tie the ends of a 12-inch string through the holes of each windsock to make the handle. Allow the children to take the windsocks outside and fly them by holding the fish up by the handles and running.

Magnet Art

Your children will have tons of fun while using magnets to create abstract works of art. Each child will need a strong magnet, a tray (plastic trays used in many school cafeterias work well), and a small metal object such as a spring. Tape a sheet of art paper to the inside of each tray. Then place small drops of bright-colored paints on the paper. Have each child place the metal object on top of the drops of paint. Next have her hold the magnet underneath the tray and move it along the bottom to create a unique design.

SNACK

Ice Cream

Pour one-half cup of milk, one-fourth teaspoon of vanilla, and one tablespoon of sugar into a pint-size Ziploc plastic bag. Seal the bag tightly. Then fill a gallon-size Ziploc bag half full of crushed ice and add one-half cup of salt. Place the pint bag inside the gallon bag and seal it. Shake the mixture about five minutes to make ice cream.

CULMINATING ACTIVITY

Energy Fair

Set up an energy fair. Let pairs of children demonstrate several simple energy experiments placed around the classroom. Invite parents or children from other classes to attend.

Energy Patterns
Use with "Cover The Sun" on page 45.

Push.

Pull.

Fairy Tales

Your children will live happily ever after in the enchanted land of fairy tales and fantasy. This focus on make-believe will involve your youngsters in many enjoyable hands-on experiences.

MATH

What's In A Name?

There are fifteen letters in the name *Rumpelstiltskin*. Write the name on the chalkboard and then count the letters. Next write the name in a grid, printing each letter in a separate box. Then have each child print her first name in a similar grid. Tell her to count the letters in her name. Have the children decide whose names have the most letters, the fewest letters, and the same number of letters. Then place their names in descending order under the name Rumpelstiltskin. To vary the activity, let your children write their first and last names in separate grids. Tell each child to decide which of her names has more letters. Then ask her to compare the number of letters in both of her names with her classmates'.

Let Down Your Hair

How long was Rapunzel's hair? Let the children in your class discover the answer to this question while practicing estimation and measuring skills. To prepare for the activity, braid several long strands of yarn to resemble a ponytail. Secure the ends with ribbon. Show the ponytail to your children. Ask them to pretend that it is Rapunzel's hair. Then, using a nonstandard unit of measurement, have each child estimate its length. For example, it is 5 pencils long or 30 Duplo blocks long. Ask each child to write his estimation on a slip of paper. Then have your students sit in a circle. Lay the braid on the floor and measure it. Write the actual measurement on the board and have your children compare their estimations to see which child was the closest.

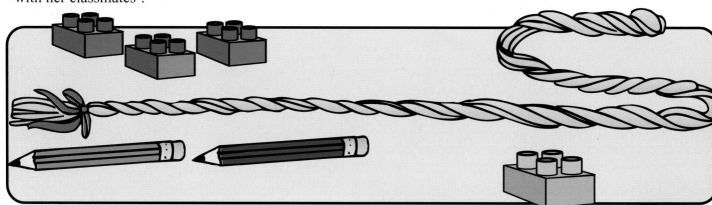

Sizing Up Teddies

After reading *Goldilocks And The Three Bears,* discuss size relationships (small, medium, and large) with your youngsters. Then have your students bring in teddy bears from home. Allow students to line up the teddy bears starting with the smallest and going to the biggest bear.

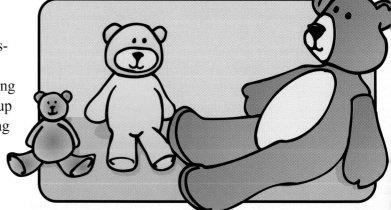

If The Shoe Fits

Read the story *Cinderella* to your class. Then ask your youngsters to describe the characteristic that made Cinderella's shoes special. Afterwards let the children participate in a sorting activity and compare shoes. Place a Hula-Hoop on the floor. Ask each child to put her shoe inside it (teacher, too). Lay a second Hula-Hoop beside the first. Have a student volunteer sort the shoes into two groups using an attribute such as *tie/no tie, color,* or *the size of the heel.* Then ask the remaining members of the class to decide which attribute was used for sorting. Repeat the activity several times with other student volunteers.

One Hundred Kisses

The wolf is the villain in *Little Red Riding Hood* and *The Three Little Pigs*. However, in *The Wolf's Chicken Stew* by Keiko Kasza, the wolf has a change of heart and receives one hundred kisses from a family of baby chicks. Read this delightful story to your children. Then place several containers of small objects such as pom-poms or candy kisses in a learning center. Have your students help each other count one hundred items from each of the containers.

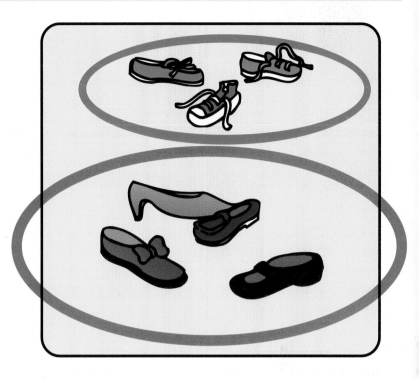

The Seven Dwarfs

The seven dwarfs from the Walt Disney version of *Snow White* can be easily recognized by children. Obtain a picture of each dwarf from a coloring book or poster. Glue each picture to a separate square of tagboard for durability. Teach the dwarfs' names to your children. Then place the pictures in a row on a chalkboard ledge. Ask the children to name the dwarf that is third, fifth, second, etc. Then change the order of the pictures and repeat the activity. Next have each child decide which dwarf is his favorite. Place the pictures in a row on the floor. Then give each child a block or a Unifix cube and ask him to place it above the picture of his favorite dwarf. Count the number of blocks in each stack to determine which dwarf is the class favorite.

Run, Run, As Fast As You Can

After reading *The Gingerbread Boy*, give each child a copy of the reproducible on page 62. Tell him to connect the dots to create his own Gingerbread Boy.

LANGUAGE ARTS

Real And Make-Believe

There are many aspects of fairy tales that are imaginary. Talk about the differences in something real and something make-believe. Then discuss some of the make-believe people, places, and things in various fairy tales. Next ask your youngsters to cut out pictures of real and imaginary things from old magazines. Attach two large sheets of poster paper to a wall or chalkboard. Label one "Real" and the other "Make-Believe." Let each child glue his pictures to the corresponding poster.

Character Hunt

Select two characters from each of ten to twelve fairy tales. Write the name of each character on an index card. (For younger children, paste a picture of each character on a card.) Give each child a card and have him read the name of the character. Then ask him to walk around the room and find the classmate with the name of another character from the same fairy tale. Tell the pairs to sit together on the floor until everyone has found his partner.

ABC Beanstalk

Make a giant beanstalk from strips of green construction paper. Then use a leaf pattern to make twenty-six green leaves. Write an uppercase letter on the front of each leaf and a lowercase letter on the back. Place the beanstalk on the floor in the classroom. Let a small group of children work together to arrange the uppercase and then the lowercase letters in alphabetical order.

Compare And Contrast

Read the traditional versions of *Little Red Riding Hood*, *Goldilocks And The Three Bears*, and *The Three Little Pigs* aloud to your children. Then read *Lon Po Po: A Red-Riding Hood Story From China* translated by Ed Young, *Deep In The Forest* by Brinton Turkle, and *The True Story Of The 3 Little Pigs By A. Wolf* as told to Jon Scieszka. Compare and contrast these new versions with the familiar tales by making a list of how the pairs are the same and another list of how they are different. Then place a copy of each fairy tale on a table in the classroom. Let each child indicate the version she liked best by placing a teddy bear counter beside the book.

Finger-Nose Puppets

Make several copies of the reproducible on page 63 on white construction paper. Give a copy to each child in a small group. Tell him to color the puppets and cut them out on the solid lines. To hold a puppet, have him put his index finger through the hole. Then let him use the puppets to tell the story of *Goldilocks And The Three Bears*. Note: Help by cutting out the circle in the center of each puppet.

Happily Ever After

Read *The Frog Prince* to your children. Then talk about what happened to the prince and princess after they were married. Next read *The Frog Prince, Continued* by Jon Scieszka. Discuss how the writer continued the fairy tale. Then brainstorm several ideas for continuing another fairy tale such as *Sleeping Beauty* or *The Elves And The Shoemaker*. Choose one of the ideas and help your children develop a story line. Print the story on chart paper as it is dictated by the children. Then assign each child part of the story to copy and illustrate. Bind the pages together to create a class book.

Who Am I?

After reading aloud several fairy tales, ask your children several trivia questions such as those listed below.

I slept for one hundred years after pricking my finger on a spindle. Who am I? *(Sleeping Beauty)*

I was locked up in a tall tower by an old witch. Who am I? *(Rapunzel)*

I traded my cow, Milky White, for magic beans. Who am I? *(Jack)*

I was placed in a glass coffin after eating a poisoned apple. Who am I? *(Snow White)*

I retrieved a golden ball from a fountain for a princess. Who am I? *(The Frog Prince)*

I spun straw into gold for the miller's daughter. Who am I? *(Rumpelstiltskin)*

I took food to my sick grandmother. Who am I? *(Red Riding Hood)*

I changed a pumpkin into a beautiful carriage. Who am I? *(Cinderella's fairy godmother)*

Teeny-Tiny Theater

Collect small toys, puppets, or cutouts that resemble the characters from several fairy tales. Place each set of items in a container with a lid. Label each container with the name of the fairy tale. For example, for *Goldilocks And The Three Bears*, place three toy bears and a doll with blond hair in an empty coffee can or oatmeal box. Then use the toys in a container to tell a story. Afterwards return the toys to the container. Ask a child to describe the order in which the characters appeared in the story. Let the child take the items out of the container as he describes the sequence. Display the container in a learning center. Let the children in the center use it to tell the story to each other. Repeat the activity with another container of story manipulatives.

SCIENCE

Magic Water

Fairy tales have many magical and mystical elements. Your students will enjoy this fun-filled activity while making magic water. For each child in a small group, place one tablespoon of water in a bowl. Add three drops of food coloring and mix well. Then fill a baby food jar with mineral oil. Use an eyedropper to add two or three drops of colored water to the oil. Secure the lid tightly. Then tip the jar in different directions and watch the magic water float.

Hocus-Pocus

Tell your children you have a magic paper towel that can stay dry in water. Crumple a paper towel into a ball and place it in the bottom of a glass. Push the glass, open end first, straight down into a container of water. (Make sure the glass does not tilt.) Then lift the glass out of the water and remove the paper towel. Tell your children the paper towel stayed dry because the air in the glass did not let the water touch it. Return the paper-towel ball to the glass and insert the glass into the water again. This time tilt the glass so air bubbles can escape. Lift the glass out of the water, remove the paper towel from the glass, and feel the wet towel.

Abracadabra

Here's another magical activity to stir up interest in your class. Give each child in a small group two sugar cubes, two stirring sticks, a cup of warm water, and a cup of cold water. Tell the children they will watch a race between warm water and cold water to see which one can melt a sugar cube first. Before the race begins, let each child predict the winner. Then give a signal and ask each child to place one sugar cube in the cup of warm water and one in the cup of cold water. Have him stir both cups of water with the stirring sticks until one of the cubes dissolves completely. Discuss the results of the race. Ask the children to tell why one sugar cube dissolved faster than the other.

What Big Eyes You Have!

When Little Red Riding Hood saw the wolf lying in her grandmother's bed, she was surprised at her large ears, eyes, and teeth. Each child will enjoy making small objects look bigger with this simple activity. Cut the bottom out of an oatmeal box. Then cut two openings in the box near the bottom as shown. Place a piece of plastic wrap loosely over the top of the box. Secure the plastic wrap with a rubber band. Press the center of the plastic wrap in slightly to form a bowl. Fill the bowl with water. Then slide a small object through an opening so it is inside the oatmeal box, and look at it through the water. The object will be magnified.

SOCIAL STUDIES

Stranger Danger

Red Riding Hood was almost eaten by a strange wolf on her way to Grandma's house. Hansel was locked in a cage and Gretel had to work for a witch because the pair stopped at a strange house in the woods. Use these two characters to illustrate the importance of not talking to strangers and not accepting gifts from them. Then invite a representative from your local police department to present a program on stranger danger. Your school's guidance counselor may also provide your children with information on the subject.

Secret Pal

In the story *The Elves And The Shoemaker,* a pair of elves secretly helps a poor shoemaker and his wife. Read the story to your children. Discuss the story. Then talk about what it means to be a secret pal. Ask your children if they would like collectively to be a secret pal to another class for one week. Ask your children to suggest things they could do secretly for the other class. Each day, leave something made by your children outside the other class's door. On the last day of the activity, let your youngsters reveal their identity to their secret pals.

Manners Party

When Goldilocks visited the home of the Three Bears, she did not use good manners. She entered the house without being invited, ate their food without asking, broke a chair, and made a mess in every room. Discuss how Goldilocks should have behaved. Then ask the children to pretend they have been invited to the Three Bears' house for a manners party. Talk about how children should act at the party. Help them make a list of manners, similar to those listed below, on a sheet of chart paper. Then show each child how to prepare her place setting correctly using a plate, a cup, plastic utensils, and a napkin. Place baskets of snack foods on each table and let the party begin!

Manners To Remember

Place a napkin in your lap before eating.
Use the napkin to wipe your face and hands.
Do not reach for food. Ask that it be passed to you.
Use the words *please* and *thank you.*
Do not talk with food in your mouth.

Fairy Tales

ART

Magic Wand

Each child in a small group can create a magic wand with a few materials and a little imagination. Give each child a cardboard tube (such as a paper-towel tube) approximately twelve inches in length. Have him paint the surface of the tube with bright-colored paint. Then trace a star pattern on construction paper and cut it out. Decorate the star with markers, stickers, or glitter. Then flatten one end of the cardboard tube and staple the star to it. Complete the wand by attaching crepe-paper streamers or ribbon to the tube at the base of the star.

Weaving

Fairy tales such as *Rumpelstiltskin* and *The Emperor's New Clothes* include characters who can weave. Show your children how they too can become weavers with this simple activity. Cut several circles from heavy cardboard. Draw a circle in the center of each cardboard circle. Then draw eight lines that extend from the center circle to the edge of the cardboard. Cut along each of the straight lines using an X-acto knife. Give each child in a small group one of these cardboard circles. Let her paint the center with bright colored paint. Allow the paint to dry. Then have her secure a piece of yarn to the back of the circle with tape. Ask her to weave the yarn on the cardboard circle by pulling the yarn through the cuts in an over-and-under fashion. Secure the end of the yarn to the back of the circle when the weaving is complete.

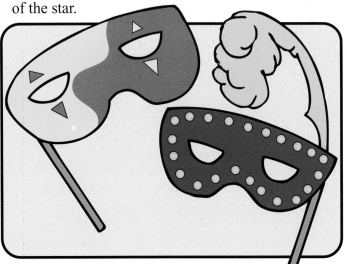

Lint Mask

Perhaps several guests who attended the ball in the story *Cinderella* wore this type of mask. To make a mask, stir three cups of dryer lint or cotton balls together with two cups of water in a large saucepan. Add two-thirds cup of flour and stir well. Add three drops of oil of cloves to the mixture. Cook over low heat. Stir until the mixture forms a peak. Pour out and let it cool on waxed paper. Shape in the form of a half-mask. Then place the top of a wooden dowel in one side of the mask. Wrap the corner of the mask over the dowel. Let dry for three to five days. Paint the mask and add sequins, feathers, and beads. Note: Approximately four masks can be made using this recipe.

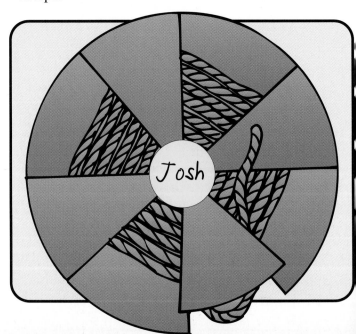

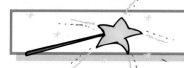

SNACK

Candy Jewels

Once the old witch was dead, Hansel and Gretel filled their pockets with her gold, silver, and precious jewels. Let each child in a small group make a candy necklace or bracelet representative of the witch's jewelry. Have her string four or five Fruit Loops on a licorice string. Then tie it around her neck or wrist.

CULMINATING ACTIVITY

Character Day

On the last day of the unit, ask each child to come to school dressed as his favorite fairy-tale character. Have your students guess which character each child is dressed like.

Fairy Tales
Dot-To-Dot

Use with "Run, Run, As Fast
As You Can" on page 55.

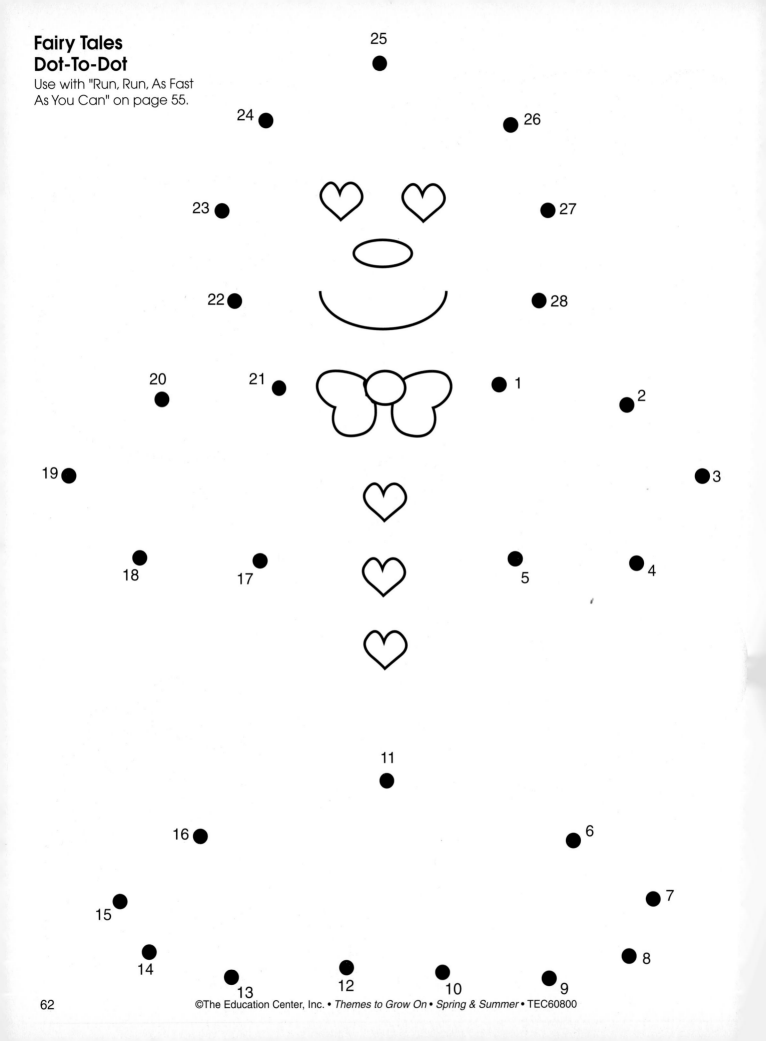

25

24   26

23   27

22   28

20   21   1   2

19   3

18   17   5   4

11

16   6

15   7

14   8

13   12   10   9

Cut this out.

Cut this out.

Cut this out.

Cut this out.

St. Patrick's Day

The luck of the Irish to you as you capture the imaginations of your youngsters with this study of leprechauns, shamrocks, potatoes, and St. Patrick.

MATH

Charm Counting

Half-fill a medium-size glass bowl with Lucky Charms cereal. Let each child estimate the number of marshmallow charms in the bowl. Write each child's estimation on a sheet of chart paper beside his name. Pour the cereal into individual paper cups. Give a cup to each child. Tell him to separate the charms from the cereal. Then ask him to sort the charms by kind. Have him count the number of charms in each group and record the number on a lab sheet. Collect the lab sheets and record the information on a class graph. Total the number of charms. Then compare the total with the estimations.

Weighing Potatoes

Place a ten-pound bag of potatoes in a learning center. Let the children in the center use a balance scale to compare the potatoes. Ask the youngsters to assist each other to determine which potato is the heaviest, which is the lightest, and which potatoes are the same.

How Many In A Handful?

Fill a widemouthed glass jar with pennies. Ask each child to reach into the jar with one hand and take out as many pennies as he can hold. Have each child estimate how many pennies he thinks he has in his hand. Record each estimation on chart paper. Then have him count his pennies. Instruct him to compare his estimated number with the actual number of pennies. Ask him to compare his answers with those of the other students in the group.

Snakes Alive!

Give each child in a small group some molding clay and a copy of the reproducible on page 72. Tell her to roll out the piece of clay equal to the length of each snake pictured on the reproducible.

Potato Eyes			
Heather	8	Janie	⑥
Carly	⑩	Maria	11
David	7	Barry	9
Grant	⑫	Sherry	⑩

Potato Eyes

What has eyes but cannot see? A potato! List each child's name on a sheet of chart paper. Give each child a potato and help her locate its eyes. Next ask each child to count the eyes on her potato. Write the number of eyes beside her name. Then, using different-colored markers, circle the greatest number, the least number, and the numbers that are the same.

mashed	fried	baked	boiled
Tim	Johnny	Pam	Diane
Keesha	Sue	Billy	
Scott	Julie	Becky	
Reggie	Kevin		

Potato Data

Have your youngsters brainstorm different ways they like to eat potatoes. Let each child make an individual graph of ways some of his classmates like to eat potatoes. Give him a copy of a grid with the headings *mashed, fried, baked, scalloped,* and *boiled* printed at the top with picture cues. Then, when he has free time during the day, let him ask five classmates how they like their potatoes cooked. Tell him to ask each child to write her name under the appropriate heading on the grid. Make sure he adds his name also. Then have him compare the data on his graph to see which type of potato was most popular among his peers. To vary the activity, make a class graph and ask each child to color in a space under the selected heading.

Shamrock Rock

Reinforce basic number concepts with this small-group game. Laminate and cut out a green, construction paper shamrock on page 73 for each player. Write a different number on each cutout; then place the shamrocks facedown on a table. While Irish music is playing, have children march around the table. When the music stops, each player picks up a shamrock. The child with the lowest number is out. Continue playing until only one child is left. For older students, write math facts on the shamrocks. The student with the lowest answer in each round is eliminated.

LANGUAGE ARTS

Leprechaun Story

Print the following story on a sheet of chart paper. Then let your children dictate the words to be printed in the blanks. Once the story is complete, copy it on poster board. Let a small group of children illustrate the story. Then display the poster in the classroom.

Once upon a time there was a leprechaun named _____.
He lived in _____. He liked to hide _____.
_____ (name of leprechaun) also liked to play tricks on grown-ups. One day he played a trick on _____(teacher or principal). He
_____
(description of trick).

ABC Money

A pot of gold in the classroom will capture the attention of your children. Cut out twenty-six coins from yellow or gold tagboard. Label each coin with an alphabet letter. Place the coins in a black pot or kettle. Ask the children to sit in a circle on the floor. Tell each child to take one coin from the pot and return to her place. When all of the coins have been removed, have the children collectively place them in alphabetical order. To vary the activity, place the pot of coins in a learning center. Ask each child in the center to take six or seven coins from the pot and arrange them in alphabetical order. Then return the coins to the pot and begin the activity again.

Hot Potato

Put a new twist on an old game. First write the word *leprechaun* on the chalkboard. Then ask your children to sit in a circle on the floor. Play an Irish record and begin passing a potato around the circle. Stop the record. Ask the child holding the potato to stand and name a word that begins with the first letter in the word *leprechaun.* If correct, the letter is erased and the game begins again using the next letter. If incorrect, the game continues using the same letter. The game is over when all the letters in *leprechaun* have been erased. To extend play, use other words such as *rainbow, shamrock,* and *potato.*

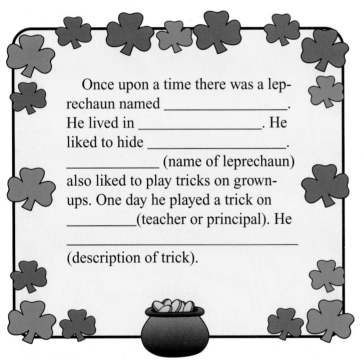

GREEN THINGS

A plant is green.

A globe is green.

Green Eggs And Ham

Read aloud *Green Eggs And Ham* by Dr. Seuss. Then brainstorm a list of green things with your class. Write them on your chalkboard. Next have each child make an individual book titled "Green Things." Prepare the pages ahead of time by printing, "A _____ is green," at the bottom of each one. Then staple three pages inside a green cover for each child. Ask her to copy a different word from the list in each of the blanks and illustrate the completed sentences. Prepare a snack of green eggs and ham while your children are working on their books. You will need an electric skillet, utensils, eggs, ham, and green food coloring.

Magic Poems

Make an interactive chart using Shel Silverstein's poem "Magic" from *Where The Sidewalk Ends.* Print the poem on a sheet of chart paper. Then print each child's name on a separate strip of tagboard. Teach the poem to your youngsters. Then place the chart and the name cards in a learning center. Let the children choose six name cards, place them over names of the people in the poem, and read the poem.

Pot Of Gold

What would you do with a leprechaun's pot of gold? Would you buy a toy store or a truckload of candy? Would you put it in the bank or give it to someone who really needed it? Lead your class in a discussion of ways to use a leprechaun's gold pieces. List each suggestion on a sheet of chart paper. Then give each child a sheet of paper with the sentence, "If I found a leprechaun's pot of gold, I'd _____," printed at the bottom. Ask him to complete the sentence and illustrate it. Then bind the pages together to create a class book.

Shamrock Concentration

Make a versatile shamrock gameboard and use it to practice a variety of skills. Cut a large shamrock from green poster board. Draw 24 circles on the gameboard. Label 12 wooden, plastic, or paper disks with some uppercase letters of the alphabet. Label 12 other disks with matching lowercase letters of the alphabet. Place the gameboard and its pieces in a learning center.

To play, place all the disks facedown on the gameboard, one disk per circle. In turn, each player turns over two disks. If they match, the player keeps the disks and takes another turn. If there is no match, the disks are turned back over and it is the next player's turn. The player with the most disks at the end of the game wins.

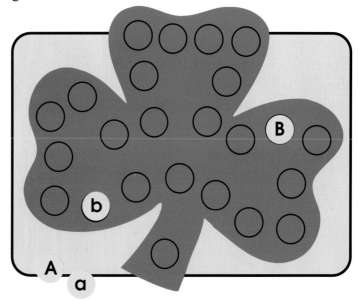

67

SCIENCE

Balloon Tricks

Leprechauns love to play tricks on people. Your children will love to watch these simple balloon demonstrations. For safety, remove the balloon from children's reach after the demonstration.

Rub an inflated balloon with a wool cloth. Then put the balloon against a wall and it will stick. Rub the balloon with the wool cloth again. Then use it to pick up small pieces of paper.

Put a piece of transparent tape on a balloon. Then insert a pin through the tape and the balloon. The balloon will not pop. When the pin is removed, however, it will go down slowly.

Have a student volunteer use a bubble pipe to blow a bubble. Ask him to hold the bubble on the pipe. Then rub a balloon with a wool cloth. Hold the balloon close to the bubble, and the bubble will bend toward the balloon.

Emerald Dust

Place a carton of milk, a container of magic emerald dust (instant powdered pistachio pudding), and several empty baby food jars on a table in a learning center. Let each child in the center pour one-fourth cup of milk in a jar. Then have him add 1 1/2 teaspoons of emerald dust to the milk. Tell him to secure the lid tightly and shake the jar until the mixture changes into pudding. Then eat and enjoy!

Capture The Leprechaun

For homework, ask each child to design and build a leprechaun catcher. On the following day, let him demonstrate his leprechaun trap to the rest of the class. To vary the activity, let each child draw a picture of a leprechaun catcher. Then write a description of the catcher, as it is dictated by the child, at the bottom of the page. Bind the pages together to create a class book titled "How To Catch A Leprechaun."

SOCIAL STUDIES

Friendship Plant

The shamrock is a three-leafed plant that resembles clover and grows freely in Ireland. Use this cheerful, decorative plant to foster friendship in your classroom. Purchase a large shamrock plant and small pots for this activity. Then gently pull the shamrock apart and give each child a piece to plant in a pot. Explain that when the shamrock outgrows the pot, each child should separate the plant and share the plant and her friendship with someone else. If she does, friendship—like the plant—will continue to grow. Finally plant one section in a pot and keep it in the classroom.

Wearing Of The Green

Why do we wear green on St. Patrick's Day? Green is the symbol of nature. Ireland, the Emerald Isle, is covered with beautiful green grass and foliage in the springtime, making green a special color for the Irish people. Ask your children to wear green on St. Patrick's Day or on the last day of this unit, in honor of the Irish people.

Ireland

Set up a center in your classroom where your children can learn more about Ireland. Attach a map to the wall and place a marker on Ireland. Also include books, magazine articles, and pictures of Ireland and its people. Finally hang a flag or drawing of the flag in the center.

Islands

An island is a landmass surrounded by water. Show your children a picture of Ireland and explain that it is an island country. Then show your youngsters several maps and have them locate other islands. Mark each one with a pin or sticker.

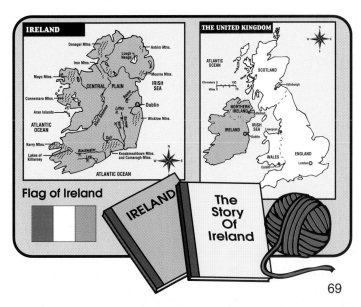

ART

Rainbow Colors

Place a bowl of liquid starch, white paper, paint-brushes, and individual bowls of powdered tempera paint in a learning center. Tell each child to use a paintbrush to cover a sheet of paper with liquid starch. Then have him dip a damp paintbrush into one of the bowls of powdered paint and dab it onto the paper. The starch will change the powder into a thick paint. Repeat the procedure with other colors of powdered tempera to make a colorful design.

Green On Green

Give each child in a small group a sheet of green construction paper. Ask her to use a crayon that is a different shade of green to draw a picture on the paper. Then let her paint over the picture with diluted white tempera paint. The paint will be absorbed by the paper and resisted by the crayon.

Snake Art

Legend has it that St. Patrick drove all the snakes out of Ireland. Let your children look at books about snakes and observe the snakes' beautiful colors and designs. Then give each child a large sheet of paper. Tell her to use a pencil to draw the outline of a snake on the paper. Next have her use paint or markers to make colorful patterns on the snake's body. Trace around the snake with a black marker. Then cut out the snakes and attach them to a bright-colored background.

Leprechaun Finders

Trying to spy a leprechaun will be loads of fun with this decorative finder. Have each child in a learning center paint a small cardboard tube with bright-colored tempera paint. When the paint has dried, let her attach sequins, beads, and stickers to the tube. Then secure a square of green plastic wrap to one end of the tube using a rubber band. Now she is ready to begin a leprechaun hunt!

SNACK

Pudding In A Cloud

1 8-oz. tub Cool Whip, thawed
2 cups cold milk
1 small package Jell-O instant pudding,
  any flavor
rainbow-colored candy sprinkles

Pour milk into a medium bowl. Add pudding mix. Beat with wire whisk for one to two minutes. Let stand for five minutes. Spoon Cool Whip evenly into six clear plastic cups. Using a spoon, spread Cool Whip into the bottom and up the sides of each cup. Spoon pudding into the center of each Cool Whip "cloud." Sprinkle with rainbow-colored candy sprinkles. Yields six servings.

CULMINATING ACTIVITY

Each day of the unit, set a trap to catch a leprechaun. Then, while your class is at lunch or recess, ask a colleague to make the room look as though a leprechaun has visited it. Have her spring the trap, scatter toys around the room, overturn a few chairs, and leave a note from the leprechaun. On the final day of the unit, ask her to leave a surprise or treat—such as gold foil-wrapped chocolate coins—for your children from the leprechaun.

St. Patrick's Day

Use with "Snakes Alive!" on page 65.

©The Education Center, Inc. • *Themes to Grow On* • *Spring & Summer* • TEC60800

Water

Water, water everywhere! Help your children learn to appreciate the importance of water as they learn about its many properties.

MATH

Measuring Water

Place a water table, foam cups, funnels, and several unbreakable containers—such as a plastic soup bowl, a pitcher, a loaf pan, a butter tub, and a liter bottle—in a learning center. Ask each child in the center to choose a container and estimate how many foam cups of water it will take to fill it. Graph each child's prediction on chart paper. Then let her check the accuracy of her prediction by pouring water by the cupful into the container. Have her repeat the same procedure with other containers. Note: Let children use a funnel with containers that have small necks.

Measuring Water		
Joe-10	Joe-9	Joe-4
Alex-9	Alex-8	Alex-5
Susan-9	Susan-8	Susan-6
Teri-6	Teri-7	Teri-5
Josh-7	Josh-9	Josh-7
Billy-8	Billy-6	Billy-4

How Many Drops?

How many drops of water will a penny hold? Assist a small group of children to discover the answer to this question. Give each child a penny, an eyedropper, a pencil, and a copy of the top half of the reproducible on page 82. Have her estimate the number of drops of water a penny will hold and write her estimation in the first water drop on the reproducible. Then let her perform the experiment and write the actual number of water drops the penny held in the second water drop. Repeat the experiment with a nickel, dime, or quarter.

How Far Can You Toss?

Each child will enjoy measuring the distance he can toss a wet sponge. Use long jump ropes to create boundary lines at three feet, six feet, nine feet, 12 feet, and 15 feet. Then have a small group of children form a straight line behind the boundary line. Give each child a wet sponge. Ask the first child in line to toss his sponge. Record the greatest distance tossed on a scorecard. Then let the next child in line toss her sponge. At the end of the game, see how many balloons sponges in each range.

Water Sports

Ask your children to help you create a list of water sports such as tubing, swimming, skiing, boating, fishing, and diving. Record the name of each activity on a sheet of chart paper and draw a picture cue beside it. Then ask each child to indicate which water sport is her favorite by placing a round sticker beside the appropriate name/picture cue. Compare the results of this simple graph when finished.

Buckets Of Water

Measuring water will be buckets of fun with this outdoor relay game. Divide your class into two or three teams. Place a bucket of water at each team's starting line and an empty bucket several feet away. Then give the first child in each line a small paper cup. Have him fill the cup by dipping it into the bucket of water. Tell him to hold the cup in one hand, run to the empty bucket, and pour the remaining water in it. Repeat the activity until each child has had a turn. Then measure the amount of water collected in each bucket to determine a winner.

How High Can You Count?

Use a paintbrush to paint a strip of water on the chalkboard. Then ask a student volunteer to see how high he can count before the water evaporates. Repeat the activity with other children.

School Of Fish

Make 15 copies of the fish reproducible on page 82. Cut out the fish shapes. Separate a set of ten cutouts and label each one with a numeral from one through ten. Label each of the remaining fish with a numeral from one through five. Then have a small group of children sit around a table. Place a long piece of string in the center of the table and ask the children to pretend it is a fishing line. Divide the set of ten fish among the children. Keep the set of five fish. Hold up the fish with the one printed on it and read the first sentence printed below. Let the child with the answer fish place it on the fishing line. Continue until all the fish have been placed on the fishing line.

I have 1.   Who has plus 1?   (2)
I have 2.   Who has plus 1?   (3)
I have 3.   Who has plus 5?   (8)
I have 4.   Who has plus 3?   (7)
I have 5.   Who has plus 4?   (9)
I have 1.   Who has plus 0?   (1)
I have 2.   Who has plus 2?   (4)
I have 3.   Who has plus 2?   (5)
I have 4.   Who has plus 6?   (10)
I have 5.   Who has plus 1?   (6)

Adapt this activity for younger students by reproducing 20 copies of page 82. Program ten of the fish with numerals from one to ten. Program the other fish with corresponding dots from one to ten. Give the fish with the dots to ten students. Follow the same procedure as above as you hold up a fish with a numeral and ask which child has the matching fish with the corresponding number of dots.

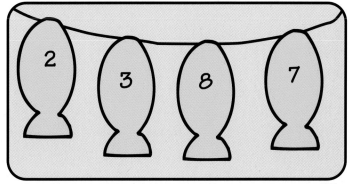

LANGUAGE ARTS

Rhyme Time

Read aloud *Sheep On A Ship* by Nancy Shaw. After discussing the book, read it a second time, stopping at the end of each page to let your children name the words that rhyme. List the rhyming words on chart paper. Then place the list in a writing center to be used as a reference.

map
nap
form
storm

lap
flap
sails
rails

ship
slip

Stand Up; Sit Down

Play a recording of the song "My Bonnie Lies Over The Ocean." Instruct your children to stand up and then sit down quickly each time they hear a word beginning with the letter *B*. Your youngsters will love the movement in this letter recognition activity.

Compound Words

Make a list of compound words that begin with *water* such as *watermelon, waterfall, waterproof,* and *waterworks*. Then make additional lists of compound words that begin with *sun, rain,* and *snow*. Next create a flip book for each child by stapling three half-sheets of paper to the right side of a sheet of construction paper. Let the child choose one set of compound words and copy "water," "sun," "rain," or "snow" on the sheet of construction paper. Then have him print three different words on the half-sheets of paper to create three compound words.

Itsy-Bitsy Spider

Print the words of the song "Itsy Bitsy Spider" on a sheet of chart paper. Read the poem aloud to your children. Point out the high-frequency words. Then print the song on a second sheet of chart paper, leaving blanks in place of the high-frequency words. Write the missing words on individual tagboard strips. Then ask your children to attach the word cards to the second chart in the appropriate blanks and read the poem. Finally let your youngsters listen to the delightful story "The Heroic Climb Of Itsy-Bitsy Spider" by David Novak, from the cassette *A Spider's Gotta Do What A Spider's Gotta Do.*

Sink And Float

After completing "Water Play" on page 78, let your children make a class book. Ask each child to dictate a sentence about one of the objects used in the activity (for example, "A rock will sink" or "A straw will float."). Print the sentences on chart paper. Then copy each sentence on a separate sheet of paper. Let each child illustrate her sentence. Then bind the pages together to create a class book titled "Sink And Float."

Poetry Box

To make a poetry box, first rinse and drain two half-gallon cardboard beverage containers. Draw a line around each container four inches from the bottom. Cut along the lines and remove the containers' tops. Then slide the containers' bottoms together to create a box. Cover the box with Con-Tact paper. Next print six water-related poems or songs such as "Jack And Jill"; "Rain, Rain, Go Away"; "It's Raining"; "Row, Row, Row Your Boat"; "I'm A Little Teapot"; and "There Is Thunder" on separate squares of paper. Attach each poem or song to one side of the poetry box. Then ask your children to sit in a circle on the floor. Play a record and pass the box around the circle. Stop the record and ask the child holding the cube to roll it on the floor. Assist the children in reciting the poem or singing the song that lands right-side up. Then begin the activity again.

Kapiti Plain

The cumulative rhyme of the African folktale *Bringing The Rain To Kapiti Plain* retold by Verna Aardema will enchant your youngsters. Read the story aloud to your class. Then let your children sequence the events that brought rain to Kapiti Plain. Place sentence strips with the sentences printed below and pictures to correlate with each sentence in random order in a pocket chart. Read the sentences aloud and ask your children to tell which one should come first. Place the appropriate sentence strip at the top of the pocket chart. Continue until all the sentences are in the correct sequence. Then have your children read the sentences with you.

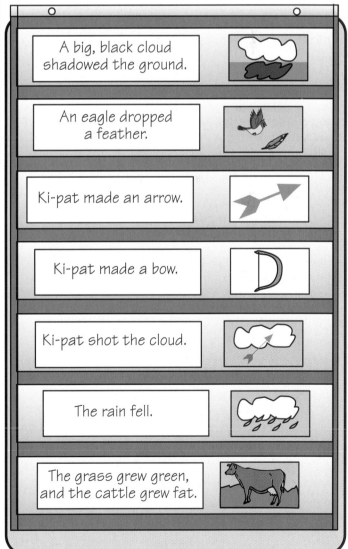

SCIENCE

Water Play

Place a water table, a container labeled "sink," and one labeled "float" in a learning center. Then put several small objects such as a Ping-Pong ball, a wooden block, a rock, a cork, a sponge, a crayon, and a straw into the water. Ask the children in the center to stand around the water table. Let one child use an aquarium fishnet to scoop up one of the objects. Have him place the object in either the container labeled "sink" or the one labeled "float." Then ask him to pass the net to another child. Continue in the same manner until all the objects have been caught. Take the objects out of the two containers and place them on a table. Then give each child a copy of the reproducible on page 83. Have him draw pictures of the objects that sank and pictures of the items that floated.

Water Shapes

Place a ball of clay in a clear glass container. Does the clay take on the shape of the container? What if you poured water into the same container? Place three different containers in a learning center. Let a child in the center fill the first container with colored water. Then ask the children to observe the shape of the water in the container. Have them use crayons to draw the shape on a sheet of paper. Repeat the activity with the other containers. Finally ask the children in the center to describe what happens to the shape of water when it is poured into a container.

The Water Cycle

The water you are drinking today could have been used by a dinosaur millions of years ago! Use the story *The Water Cycle* by Helen Frost to share how the water cycle works. Then discuss the story and let your youngsters make a class mural illustrating the water cycle.

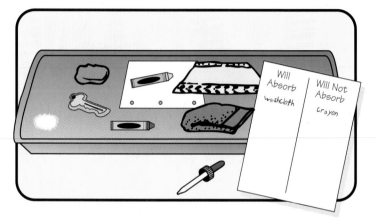

Absorption

Place several small objects such as a rock, a paper towel, a cotton ball, a key, a washcloth, a crayon, and a sheet of paper on a tray in a learning center. Ask the children to predict which of the objects will absorb water and which will not. Have them sort the objects into these two groups. Then let the youngsters use an eyedropper to place a few drops of water on each object to test which objects absorb water and which do not. Ask your students to compare their predictions to what actually happened.

Where Does It Go?

Pour materials such as sugar, salt, powdered sugar, honey, cooking oil, cornstarch, and flour into separate containers, and label each one. Place a container of plastic spoons and a quantity of baby food jars in a learning center. Let the children in the center fill the baby food jars with warm water. Then ask a child to stir a spoonful of one of the materials into a jar of water. Ask the others to observe the material and describe what they see. Repeat the activity with the other materials. Then ask the children to name the materials that will and will not dissolve in water.

SOCIAL STUDIES

Water Conservation

In some parts of the world, people must fetch water from faraway sources. In other parts of the world, drought, floods, and water shortages make it necessary for everyone to be careful with how much water is used. Lead your children in a discussion of ways they can conserve water at home and at school. Then divide the class into small groups. Ask each group to make a poster illustrating how water can be conserved. Display the posters in the classroom or in the hallway near drinking fountains and restrooms.

Water, Water Everywhere!

Lead your class in a tour throughout the school to discover ways water is used. Begin your search in the classroom. Then visit the cafeteria, teachers' lounge, principal's office, library, and other classrooms. Next help your children make a list of their findings (such as washing hands, painting with watercolors, drinking from a water fountain, cleaning with water, making coffee, watering plants, cooking lunch, etc.). For homework, tell each child to look for ways water is used at home. On the following day, let children share what they discovered with the rest of the class.

Waterworks

Where does your community gets its water? Some cities get their water from nearby lakes or rivers. Others get their water from underground sources or from melting snow. Invite a representative from the local water treatment plant to discuss the answer to this question with your children. Also have him describe the process used to clean the water. If a water treatment representative is unavailable, invite a plumber to explain how water enters a house and how dirty water is carried away.

Bodies Of Water

Use large maps to point out different bodies of water such as lakes, rivers, and oceans. Then divide the class into pairs and give each pair a small map or travel atlas. Ask the children to find similar bodies of water on their maps.

ART

Framed Fish

Your children can create beautiful paper fish that can be proudly displayed in printed frames. To make a fish, give each child two different-colored sheets of construction paper. Then demonstrate how the body of a fish can be made by using a pair of scissors and a sheet of paper. (For this activity it is not recommended that anything be drawn before it is cut out.) Also stress the importance of making the fish as large as possible. Allow your youngsters time to cut out their fish, and have them place the cutouts on the background paper when finished. Next demonstrate how to cut eyes, fins, gills, stripes, and spots from scraps of paper to decorate the fish. Tell the children not to copy your example, but to use some of their ideas to create unique fish of their own. Once everyone has completed the cutting, have them take everything off the background paper. Next show the children how to glue their fish to the background papers and body parts to the fish. (It is all right if the fish hangs over the edge of the paper; it gives the picture character.)

The final step involves making printed frames for the fish and can be completed the following day. First place several empty spools of thread on each table. (Plastic spools are best because their ends are not solid.) Place several paper plates on the tables and pour a small amount of tempera paint in each plate. Next give each child a piece of construction paper that is larger than the background sheet (there should be at least a two-inch border on all sides of the picture). Demonstrate how to center a picture on a larger sheet of paper and glue them together, allowing the children time to follow your example. Finally show the youngsters how to place the end of a spool into the paint and use it to print a design around the picture frame.

Dyeing

Let your children use food coloring to create beautiful designs on absorbent sheets of paper. Ask a small group of children to sit around a table. Place containers of food coloring on the center of the table. Then give each child a paper towel or a sheet of rice paper that has been folded into fourths or eighths. Let him dip each corner of the paper in a different container of food coloring. Then unfold the paper and let it dry. To vary the activity, let each child use an eyedropper to add spots of color to a coffee filter or paper towel.

SNACK

Edible Ocean

Make blue Jell-O according to package directions. Pour it into individual clear plastic cups. Refrigerate one hour or until set. Then top with whipped cream waves. Serve with plastic spoons.

CULMINATING ACTIVITY

Splash Party

Plan an end-of-the-week splash party outside that includes several games such as wet sponge toss. Gather several sponges, two dishpans and a bucket of water. Divide students into two teams and ask them to line up behind a tossing line. Place the two dishpans a few feet in front of the tossing line. Give the first person in each line a wet sponge and have her toss at her team's dishpan. If it goes in the pan, record a tally mark for the team. Each player continues to toss and earn marks until she misses. Then the next player tosses. Play continues until all the players from each team have had a turn. Total the tallies for each team and see how many hits the whole class scored!

Water

Use with "How Many Drops?" on page 74.

Estimation	Actual

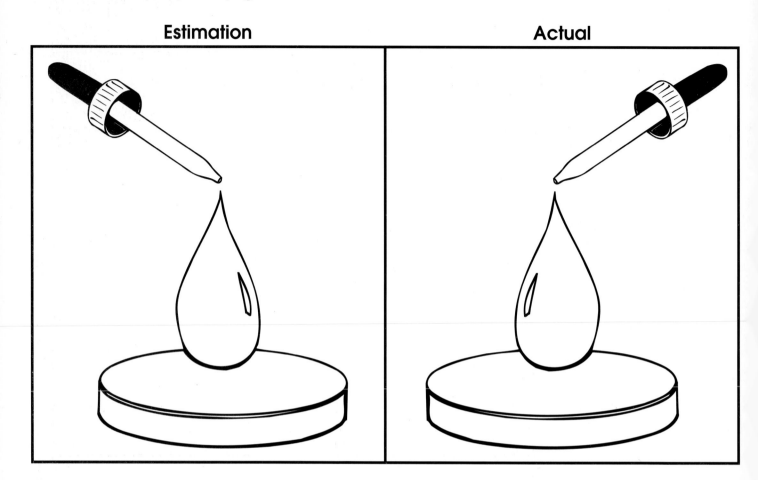

Use with "School Of Fish" on page 75.

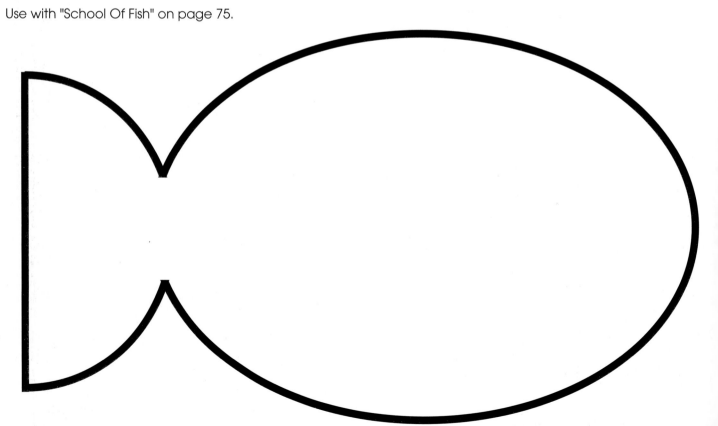

Water

Use with "Water Play" on page 78.

Float

Sink

Plants And Seeds

MATH

Excitement will sprout in your classroom with these fun-filled activities. Your youngsters will weigh, measure, sort, count, and predict as they investigate the interesting world of plants and seeds.

Lima Bean Addition

Place a piece of cardboard on the ground. Pour five to ten dried lima beans on the cardboard and spread them out evenly. Then paint one side of each bean. When the paint is dry, place the beans in a paper cup. Working with an individual child, pour the beans onto a table. Each bean will be showing a natural white surface or a painted one. Ask the child to use the two different colors of beans to show an addition equation on a sheet of paper. For example, if one white bean and four red beans were showing, the equation would be $1 + 4 = 5$. Return the beans to the cup and repeat the activity.

Bunches Of Beans

Pour several varieties of dried beans into a large resealable bag and mix them well. Then have a child in a small group sort the beans by kind.

Weighing Seeds

For this activity you will need a balance scale and a variety of seeds. Some seeds may be purchased from a local garden shop or hardware store. Other seeds—such as peach, watermelon, avocado, and apple—may be saved from the foods you eat. Place each seed type in a resealable bag. Then place the seeds and the set of scales in a learning center. To compare the different seeds, use a large seed such as a peach or an avocado as a standard of measure. For example, put a peach seed on one side of the balance scale. Then place apple seeds on the other side of the scale until it balances. Count to see how many apple seeds are needed to equal the weight of one peach seed. Repeat the activity with another type of seed.

Seed Match

Prepare five pairs of matching cards, each pair with a different seed-pattern design. Place the cards in a learning center. Let each child in the center pair the matching patterns or designs.

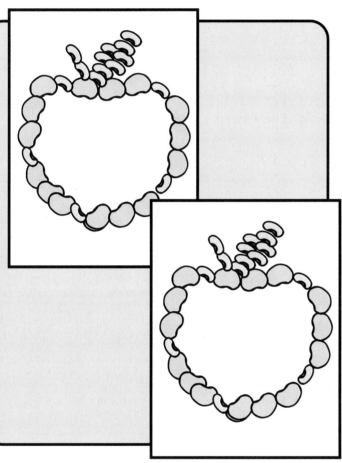

Three In A Row

Make several copies of the reproducible on page 92. Write the numerals 1 to 9 on the playing sheets in random order, making each sheet different. Then make a set of number word cards to use with the game. Give each child in a small group one of the playing sheets and paper bean cutouts. Place the word cards in a stack, facedown, in the center of the playing area. Let one child lift the top card and show it to the others in the group. Then have each child put a bean on the corresponding numeral wherever it appears on her playing sheet. Play continues until one child gets three in a row vertically, horizontally, or diagonally.

Munchy Plant Parts

Collect seed catalogs from friends, parents, or the local agricultural extension office. Then prepare a class graph of edible plant parts such as the root, stem, leaf, and flower. Give your children the seed catalogs and have them cut out pictures that show examples of foods in each category. Then glue the pictures to the graph. When the graph is complete, count the pictures in each category.

LANGUAGE ARTS

Plant Poetry

Use the poem "Maytime Magic" by Mabel Watts, from *The Random House Book Of Poetry For Children* selected by Jack Prelutsky, with several different language arts activities. First, read the poem aloud to your children. Then have them read it with you. Discuss the many things needed to make a plant grow from a seed and list them on a sheet of chart paper. Next, divide the class into small groups. Assign each group one or two lines, and have the groups perform a choral reading of the poem. Then make an interactive chart of the poem by printing it on a sheet of chart paper, omitting the words *seed, earth, hole, pat, wish, sun, shower, while,* and *flower.* Print the omitted words on individual word cards. Ask the children to read the poem and place the missing words in the appropriate spots. Finally let small groups of children take turns acting out the poem while the others read it.

Jack And The Beanstalk

Give each child a plastic sandwich bag and a copy of the reproducible on page 93. Have him cut out the pictures along the solid black lines and place them in front of him. Then read aloud the story *Jack And The Beanstalk.* As you read, ask each child to place the pictures of the people or things in the sandwich bag as they appear in the story. Afterwards have him take the pictures out of the bag and name each one in the correct sequence.

Familiar Sayings

A list of familiar sayings such as the ones listed below can be found in a farmer's almanac or in a book of quotations. Print several of these famous sayings on a sheet of chart paper. Discuss the meaning of each saying with your children. Then let each child choose one saying and draw a picture that illustrates its meaning. Bind the pictures together to create a class book or display them on a bulletin board.

　　Fresh as a daisy.
　　Sweet as a rose.
　　Everything's coming up roses.
　　Grows like a weed.
　　Soft as a petal.

In My Garden

Play the song "In My Garden" from Raffi's *One Light, One Sun* CD. Then talk about the sequence of events in the song. Play the song again and have your children act it out as they sing along.

How Many Seeds?

Give each child a piece of fruit or a vegetable. Help her open it and take out the seeds. Then give her a sheet of paper with the following sentences printed on it. Ask her to complete the sentences by filling in the blanks with the appropriate information. Then let her draw a picture of the seeds and the fruit or vegetable on the sheet of paper.

    My fruit (or vegetable) is a(n) _____.

    I see _____ seeds.

    My seeds are _____.

How Seeds Travel

Seeds travel in different ways. Seeds like the cockle-bur and beggar-ticks are called *hitchhikers*. These seeds have tiny hooks or hairs that help them cling to a person's clothing or an animal's fur. Other seeds like the dandelion and the maple have wings or silky threads that help them be carried by the wind. Still other seeds like the cranberry have air spaces inside them and can float on water. Some plants spread their own seeds when the fruit splits open. Seeds can also be eaten by animals and passed through their bodies. Finally, seeds may be deliberately spread by people when they plant seeds in their gardens.

    Share these facts with your children. Then read *The Tiny Seed* by Eric Carle or *How Seeds Travel* by Cynthia Overbeck. Have your youngsters describe the various ways seeds travel. Write the different ways on a sheet of chart paper. Then have each child choose three. Ask him to illustrate each method on a sheet of paper and write or dictate a simple sentence at the bottom of each drawing. Bind the pages together to create an individual book titled "How Seeds Travel."

SCIENCE

Plants Need Water

This is a simple experiment that will let children see how a plant takes in water and carries it to each of its parts. Select a stalk of celery that has a small stem and small leaves. Place it in a glass of water that has been tinted with red or blue food coloring. After several days the color of the water will be visible throughout the celery stalk.

Parts Of A Seed

Read *One Bean* by Anne Rockwell. Then draw a large picture of a lima bean half on a sheet of poster board. Label each part as you describe its purpose (see below).

Tiny Plant or Embryo: This part will grow into a full-size bean plant.

Plant Food: The largest part of the bean. It supplies the food for the tiny plant to grow.

Seed Coat: The outer covering that protects the tiny plant and its food until it is time for the plant to grow.

Next give each child a dried lima bean that has been soaking in water overnight. Ask him to remove the seed coat. Then have him open the bean carefully and observe the tiny plant and the plant food.

Parts Of A Plant

Follow "Parts Of A Seed" with this activity. Draw a large flowering plant on a sheet of chart paper. Then label each part as you describe its function (see below). Finally let your youngsters observe the parts of a real plant.

Roots: They hold the plant in the ground and absorb water and minerals from the ground.

Stem: It supports the plant and carries food and water to the other parts.

Leaves: They make food for the plant.

Flowers: They produce seeds.

Birdseed Sprouts

Place a moist sponge in a shallow dish and sprinkle birdseed on top. Pour a small amount of water into the dish each day, being careful not to disturb the birdseed. In a few days the seeds will sprout.

SOCIAL STUDIES

Sprouting Alfalfa Seeds

Alfalfa sprouts grow quickly and are fun for children to watch. Give each child a clear plastic cup labeled with her name. Have her pour enough seeds into the cup so the bottom is covered. Then place a piece of cheesecloth over the top of the cup and secure it with a rubber band. Every morning for the next three or four days, have her rinse the seeds and pour off the excess water. The seeds will soon begin to sprout.

Plant Uses

Read *The Giving Tree* by Shel Silverstein. Then ask your children to name each of the things the tree provided the boy. List them on a sheet of chart paper. For homework, ask each child to bring in an item that came from a plant. Then, as the children share their items with the class, make a list of the products and plants that produced them.

Community Worker

Invite a florist to talk with your class. Request that she talk about the different types of flowers she works with, describing what she must do to keep them fresh. Ask her to conclude her visit by making an arrangement of flowers for the classroom.

Field Trip

Plan a trip to a local nursery. Ask for a guided tour of the facilities. Conclude the trip by having each child plant a flower in a pot or paper cup to take home.

ART

Rainbow Of Flowers

Read *Planting A Rainbow* by Lois Ehlert. Then let your children create an attractive bulletin board with a rainbow of beautiful paper flowers. Make tagboard patterns of a stem with leaves, a petal, and a flower center. Have each child use the patterns to make a different-colored flower each day of the unit. Ask her to trace the petal pattern five times on white art paper. Then sponge-paint the petals with bright-colored tempera paint. While the paint is drying, have her trace the stem on green construction paper and the flower center on yellow paper. Cut out each piece of the flower. Next glue the stem and the petals to the flower center. Then attach all the flowers in a row to a large bulletin board. Each day add another row of flowers. By the end of the week, a rainbow of flowers will brighten your classroom.

Wood Sculpture

Let the children in your class use wood scraps to create an original abstract sculpture. Obtain wood scraps from a lumberyard, sawmill, or woodworking shop. Place the wood scraps, bottles of wood glue, masking tape, and stirring sticks in a learning center. Have each child in the center choose several scraps of wood. Then instruct him to use the stirring sticks to coat both surfaces with glue before joining two pieces together. Use masking tape to support his sculpture until the glue dries.

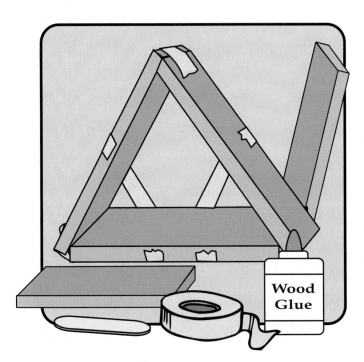

Wood Glue

Bean Bag Fun

Purchase inexpensive, bright-colored fabric and ask a parent volunteer to help you partially complete a bean bag for each child in the class. To begin, cut a rectangle from the piece of fabric. Fold the rectangle in half. Then sew up two of the sides on a sewing machine. Let each child fill a bag with dried beans, and sew up the third side using thread and an embroidery needle. To make the bag sturdier, sew the third side again on the sewing machine. Finally use the bean bags in the classroom with the *Bean Bag Activities And Coordination Skills* cassette by Georgiana Liccione Stewart and Jill Gallina.

SNACK

Sunflower Seed Candy

1 cup nonfat dry milk
1 cup honey
1 cup peanut butter (or soy nut butter)
1 cup shelled sunflower seeds
1 cup sesame seeds

Mix ingredients thoroughly. Shape into one-inch balls. Roll in sesame seeds to coat.

CULMINATING ACTIVITY

Planting A Vegetable Garden

Let each child plant a vegetable garden he can take home and watch grow. First fill a large butter tub with planting soil. Then have him plant a radish, an eye of a potato, and a carrot top in his tub. Place a radish with its sprouts in the dirt and cover half of it with the soil. Next slice an eye out of a potato that is sprouting. Place the slice in the soil so the sprout is on top and cover it with 1/4 inch of soil. Finally cut approximately one inch off the top of a sprouting carrot. Place the carrot top in the soil and cover it slightly.

Plants And Seeds

Use with "Three In A Row" on page 85.

Spring Celebration

Watch your classroom come to life with these "egg-citing" springtime activities. Your youngsters will experiment with eggs, watch baby chicks hatch, and make spring hats as they celebrate the coming of spring.

MATH

Sort And Count

Place a quantity of small spring objects such as plastic eggs, toy chicks, silk flowers, pieces of ribbon, and wrapped Easter candy in a box. Use a marker to write the name of each object on a separate sheet of construction paper. Draw a simple picture of the object beside each name for easy identification. Then put the box of objects, the labeled sheets of paper, and several paper strips in a learning center. Let the children in the center sort the spring objects and place each one on the corresponding sheet of construction paper. Ask them to count each set of objects and then write the number and name of each set of objects on a paper strip.

Simple Symmetry

Give each child a copy of the reproducible on page 102. Then have him complete the pictures of the bunny and Easter egg.

Jelly Bean Estimation

Draw the outline of a jar on a large sheet of poster board. Laminate the poster for durability. Then attach it to a wall in the classroom. Next fill two small jars with different amounts of jelly beans. Label one jar with the number of jelly beans inside. Place both jars on a small table in front of the poster. Have your youngsters carefully examine and compare the two jars of jelly beans. Then, based on her comparison, have each student estimate the number of jelly beans in the unlabeled jar. Let her use a grease pencil to write her estimation and name on the poster. At the end of the day, count the jelly beans in the unlabeled jar and decide which estimate was the closest. Repeat the activity every day of the unit, placing different amounts of jelly beans in each jar daily.

One Dozen

Set up a general store in a learning center. Place a toy cash register, paper pennies and nickels, shopping bags, and several small items such as plastic eggs, toy chicks, and wrapped candy in the center. Have the children take turns playing the customers and store clerk. Have the customers choose any combination of a dozen small items and place the items in shopping bags. Have them purchase the items from the clerk with twelve cents. Tell the clerk to count the money and the items in each shopping bag. Then ask the children to switch roles and repeat the activity.

Egg Carton Addition

Give each child in a small group an empty egg carton, a small cup of jelly beans, a pencil, and a sheet of paper. Have her place one or two jelly beans in each compartment of the egg carton. Then close the carton and shake it. Next have her open the carton and write six math equations using the positions of the jelly beans. For example, if there are three jelly beans in the top left compartment and two in the bottom left, the child would write $3 + 2 = 5$ on the sheet of paper. (Have younger students draw the two sets of jelly beans and then count the total of the two sets.) Once the six equations have been written, close the carton, shake it, and begin the activity again.

Egg Timer

Have the children in a small group sit in a circle. Give each child a plastic spoon. Designate one child as the starter and give her a plastic egg. Have the children pass the egg around the circle clockwise several times using only their spoons. Then ask one child to time the activity with a three-minute timer. Have him count the number of times the egg is passed around the circle in a three-minute period. When the game is over, choose another child to be the starter and one to be the timer, and begin again.

LANGUAGE ARTS

It's Spring

Read aloud *The Tale Of Peter Rabbit* by Beatrix Potter. Then give each child a strip of paper that has been folded into fourths. Have her use colored pencils to draw pictures showing the sequence of events from the story. Young children may draw on one side of the paper. Older children may use both sides. One note: This activity may be given as a homework assignment to allow more time for individual creativity.

Spring Words

Fold a quantity of 9" x 12" sheets of construction paper in half. Then assign each child in a small group a different spring word. Have him write the word on the left side of the paper and illustrate it. On the right side, have him list three to five words that describe the spring word and picture. Print the words for younger children.

hop
tail
ears
nose
pink
fur
carrot

carrot
ear

pretty
small

flower

Easter
colorful
painted

egg

ABC Bunny Words

Help your children brainstorm several bunny words such as *hop, tail, ears, nose, pink, fur, carrot, bunny, lettuce, rabbit, garden, jump, whiskers,* and *vegetables*. Write the words on a large bunny cutout as they are dictated. Then copy each word on an individual word card along with a picture cue, and place the cards in a learning center. Have the children in the center put the bunny words in alphabetical order using the first letter.

Springtime Journal

Make a journal for each child by stapling five sheets of white paper inside a bright-colored paper cover. Each day have her use the journal to record the date and at least one sign of spring observed that day. Let younger children draw pictures of their daily observations.

Jennie's Hat

Read aloud *Jennie's Hat* by Ezra Jack Keats. Have your children name all of the things in the book that Jennie uses as a hat. Print the name of each object in the correct order on a sheet of chart paper. Next have your youngsters name the objects brought by the birds to decorate Jennie's hat. List the name of each in the correct order on the same sheet of chart paper. Then demonstrate how each child can make a hat using two strips of wrapping paper or newsprint (see "Spring Bonnet" on page 100).

Missing Letters

Give each child a copy of the worksheet on page 103. Have her fill in the missing letters of the alphabet.

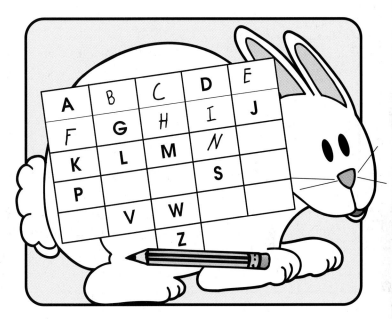

Spring Categories

Have your children think of items that belong in the following categories. List each item under the appropriate heading. Then make several blank booklets by stapling three white pages inside each bright-colored paper cover. Place the booklets and the lists in a learning center. Let each child in the center choose a booklet and a category. Have him copy the name of the category on the front cover. Then, on each page of the booklet, have him copy the name of one item in the category and draw a picture of it. Leave the booklets in the center until all of them are complete.

Things That Hop
Things That Bloom
Things With Fur
Things With Whiskers
Things That Are Sweet
Things That Are Soft
Things With Feathers
Things That Hatch

SCIENCE

Vinegar Egg

Place a raw egg in a glass container filled with vinegar. Seal the container tightly. The vinegar will slowly dissolve the calcium shell and rubberize the egg. Have your children observe the changes in the egg daily. In approximately two days, the shell will begin to soften and disappear. On the third day, take the egg out of the vinegar and let your youngsters hold it. The shell will be completely dissolved, and the egg will look and feel like a balloon filled with jelly.

Spring Walk

Take a nature walk with your children. Have them look for animals, flowers, trees, insects, and signs of spring while on the walk. When you return to the classroom, ask each child to draw a picture of one thing she saw outside. When your youngsters have finished their drawings, let them share what they saw with the others in the classroom. Bind the drawings together to create a class book or use them to make an attractive bulletin-board display called "Signs Of Spring."

Hatching Baby Chicks

Hatching baby chicks in the classroom requires a lot of work, but it is well worth the effort. It is guaranteed to be an experience your children will never forget. To begin, contact your local agricultural agent to borrow an incubator. He can also tell you where to buy fertilized eggs for the experiment and give you the information needed to successfully hatch the chicks.

SOCIAL STUDIES

We've Changed!

After discussing the many changes that occur during spring, let your children participate in an activity to see how they have changed. Ask each child to bring a baby picture from home. Post the baby pictures on a bulletin board. Then write each child's name on a strip of tagboard and place the strips in a container. Let small groups of students take turns matching names to faces. Have the children use thumbtacks to attach the name cards under the pictures. Then return the names to the container when the group has finished so another group can have a turn. Finally assemble the youngsters around the bulletin board and let each child match her name to her baby picture.

Egg Roll

One of the oldest Washington D.C. traditions is the egg-rolling event held on Easter Monday on the South Lawn of the White House. The event was first held on the grounds of the Capitol. Each year children came to test their rolling skills. However, during the Hayes administration, several congressmen grew tired of the mess created by the egg roll and banned it from the Capitol grounds. President and Mrs. Hayes invited the children to come to the White House and the egg roll has since remained a tradition.

After sharing this brief history of the event, let your children participate in their own egg-rolling contest. Have each child decorate a hard-boiled egg. Then take your children outside to the playground. Mark off a starting line and a finish line. Divide the class into several small groups. Have each child in a small group place his egg at the starting line and roll it with his hands to the finish line. The child who crosses the finish line first is the winner. Repeat the activity for each small group. Then let the winners compete against each other to determine a class egg-rolling champion.

Chris   Hannah   Amanda

ART

Bunny Ears

Let each child make a pair of bunny ears to wear for the Bunny Party (see page 101). Place scissors, pink tempera paint, sponges, a paper puncher, white construction paper, bunny ear patterns, and several plastic headbands in a learning center. Have each child trace two ear patterns on white construction paper and then cut them out. Then sponge-paint the inside of each ear pink. At the bottom of each ear, punch two holes large enough for the headband to go through. Then thread the headband through the four holes.

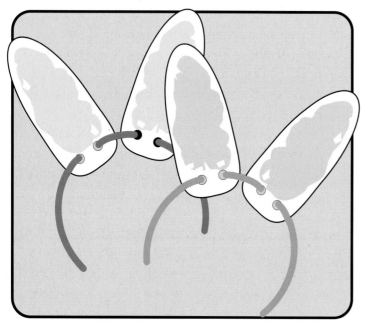

Spring Bonnet

Cut two 2-foot strips from wrapping paper or newsprint. Lay the strips of paper over the child's head in the form of a cross. Then wrap masking tape around the outside of the paper at the crown of the head. Next begin at one end of the paper and roll tightly toward the masking tape. Continue around the hat until all four sides have been rolled up to form a brim. Wrap and glue a strip of construction paper or a piece of crepe paper around the masking tape to make a hatband. Then decorate the hat with a variety of materials such as sequins, feathers, and paper flowers.

Torn-Paper Bunny

Your children will enjoy making fuzzy bunnies using torn paper. Place colored paper, glue, tagboard squares, several tin can lids of various sizes, and fine-line markers in a learning center. Let each child choose a large lid and a small one. Have him place one lid on a small piece of colored paper and tear the paper around the outside edge to create a circle. Repeat the procedure with the second lid. Then glue the two circles on a piece of tagboard to make the body of the bunny. Tear paper ears and a tail, and glue the features to the bunny's body. Use a fine-line marker to draw the whiskers. Chicks, ducklings, and other spring animals can be made using the same procedure.

Springtime Butterfly

Your youngsters will flitter and flutter when making these colorful springtime butterflies. To make a butterfly, supply each student with white construction paper. Have him draw or trace an outline of a butterfly, using as much of the paper as possible. Spray thinned tempera paint from a spray bottle over the butterfly drawing. Allow the paint to dry. Have the student cut out the butterfly. Hang these delightful works of art in your classroom.

SNACK

Bunny Bread

Prepare a loaf of frozen bread dough. Let the dough thaw. Then divide it in half. Shape one half into a flattened circle for the bunny's body and place it on a lightly greased cookie sheet. Divide the second half into two equal parts. Use one half to make the bunny's head and place next to the body. Then use the remainder to make the ears and tail. Cover and let rise for approximately 20 minutes. Then bake at 400 degrees for 18 minutes.

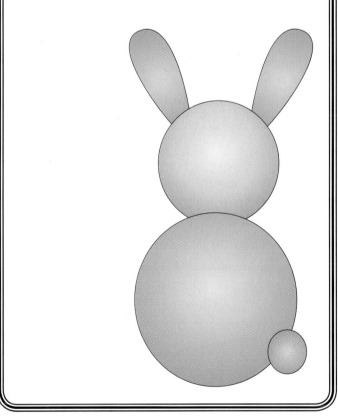

CULMINATING ACTIVITY

Bunny Party

Begin the party by playing the game Bunny Relay. Program a chart as shown giving a picture cue for which bunny facial part comes first, second, etc. Divide the class into groups of six. Post the chart so all teams can see it. Then draw a bunny body on the chalkboard for each team for the children to use as a guide. Next have each team line up single file approximately ten feet from the chalkboard. Give the first child on each team a piece of chalk. Simultaneously have each of these children hop on both feet to the chalkboard and draw a circle to make the bunny's head. The first player then hops back to his team and hands the chalk to the next child. The next team member draws the bunny ears. Play continues until each part of the bunny's face is drawn in order. The team that completes the drawing first is the winner. Afterwards have each child don his bunny ears (from "Bunny Ears" on page 100); then serve refreshments such as carrot sticks, celery with peanut butter, and orange drink.

Spring Celebration Patterns

Use with "Simple Symmetry" on page 94.

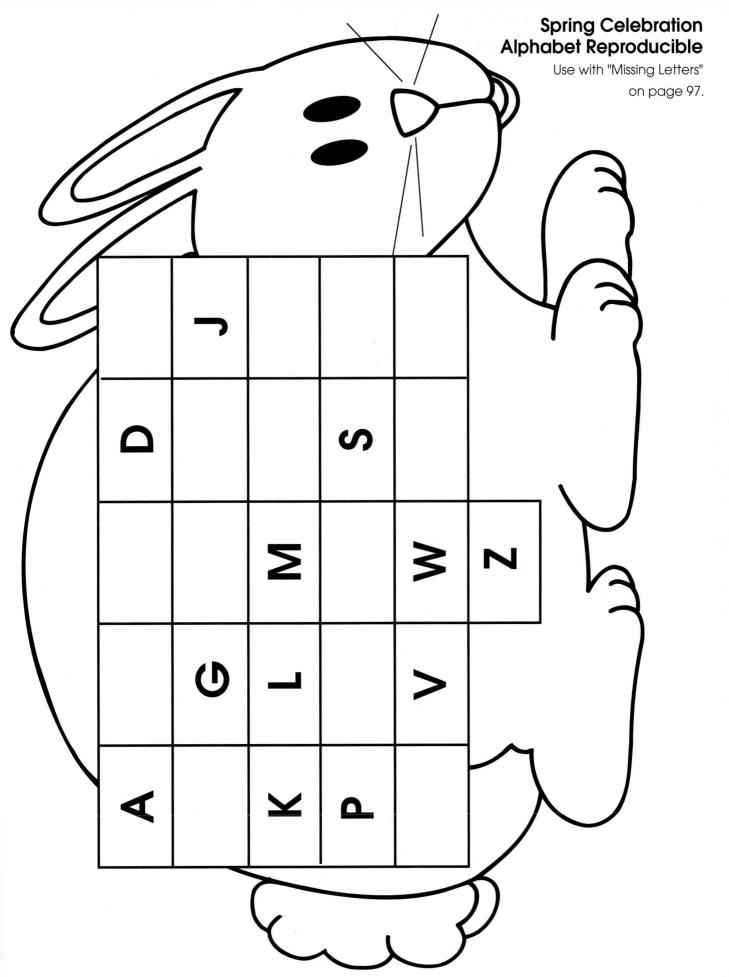

Rocks, Sand, And Soil

Dig deep into this unit to uncover the mysteries of rocks, sand, and soil. Your youngsters will have opportunities to collect, study, and discover the many uses of these materials.

MATH

Rock Sorters

Make these simple devices to help your children sort rocks of various sizes. First collect three shoeboxes. Cut a large hole in one box lid, a medium-sized hole in another, and a small hole in the remaining lid. Replace the lids on the boxes and label them "large," "medium," and "small," respectively. Place the shoeboxes and a container of rocks in a learning center. Let the children in the center use the rock sorters to separate the rocks by size. Then tell the youngsters to count the rocks in each box.

Sand Race

Color code three or four different-sized funnels. Place the funnels, detergent scoops, and a sand table in a learning center. Let each child choose a funnel and hold it over the sand table. Tell him to fill a detergent scoop with sand. Then give a signal and have him pour the sand through the funnel. Determine the order in which the funnels emptied the sand. Then let the children exchange funnels and repeat the activity several times to test the results. Finally have the youngsters put the funnels in order from fastest to slowest.

Heavy As A Rock

Place a balance scale, teddy bear counters, copies of the lab sheet on page 112, and four rocks of different sizes in a learning center. Have the children in the center estimate the weights of the rocks by putting them in order from heaviest to lightest. Next tell the youngsters to place the heaviest rock on one side of the scale and enough teddy bear counters to balance it on the other. Then have each child draw a picture of the rock in the left-hand column of a lab sheet and write the number of teddy bear counters used in the right-hand column. Instruct the children to repeat the procedure with the remaining rocks. Then have them compare the results to check their estimations.

104

Rock Bath

Help your youngsters sharpen their prediction and observation skills with this rock and water activity. Fill four clear plastic containers with colored water. Attach a ruler to the side of each container with clear Con-Tact paper. Place the containers and a set of rocks of different sizes and weights in a learning center. Let the children in the center experiment with the rocks by placing them in the containers to see how far the water will rise. Then ask the group the following questions:

Which rock made the water rise the highest? Why?

What happened when all of the rocks were placed in one container?

What happened when only the little rocks were removed? Why?

Stepping-Stones

Cut stone shapes from several sheets of gray or brown construction paper. Write a simple addition or subtraction problem with picture cues on each cutout, omitting the answer. Attach the cutouts to the classroom floor with clear Con-Tact paper to resemble stones in a stream. Then let a small group of children take turns crossing the stream. Ask a child to step on the first stone and tell the answer to the problem. If her answer is correct, she may go to the next stone. If it is incorrect, she must go back to the beginning and wait for another turn. Each child who crosses the stream is a winner.

Number Rock

Play "The Number Rock" by Greg and Steve from the *We All Live Together: Volume 2* CD. Let your children become familiar with the song. Then give each child a card labeled with a numeral from one to twenty. Play the song again. Ask each child to stand when he hears his numeral. Have your youngsters exchange number cards between verses and repeat the activity. To vary the activity, substitute number word cards for the number cards.

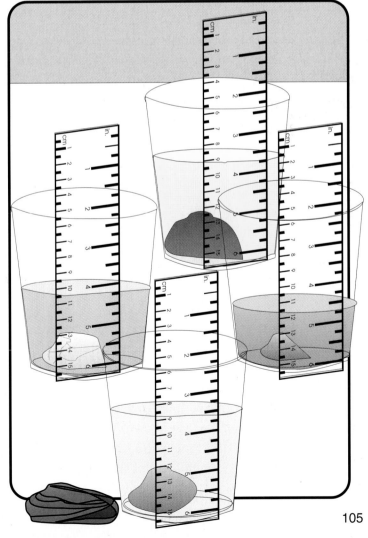

LANGUAGE ARTS

Rhymes With Rock

Print the word *rock* at the top of a sheet of chart paper. Then have your children think of words that rhyme with *rock*. Print the rhyming words on the chart paper. Then copy them on individual strips of paper. Place the word cards in a hard hat. Let a small group of children take turns drawing a card out of the hat and reading the rhyming word.

rock

clock

sock

dock

lock

The Green Grass

Read aloud "The Green Grass Grew All Around" from *On Top Of Old Smoky: A Collection Of Songs And Stories From Appalachia* compiled and adapted by Ronald Kidd. Then attach a long length of paper to a wall or chalkboard. Draw a picture of a hole in the ground on the paper. Ask your youngsters to tell what was planted in the hole. Draw a picture of a tree. Continue the process until each object has been illustrated in sequence on the strip of paper. Finally lead your children in singing "The Green Grass Grew All Around" from the accompanying cassette tape.

An earthworm lives under the ground. His home is dark and cool. He sees ants and bugs and rocks and roots.

Under The Ground

Read the poem "Under The Ground" by Rhoda W. Bacmeister from *Read-Aloud Rhymes For The Very Young* selected by Jack Prelutsky. Then ask your children to brainstorm answers to the following questions:

Where does an earthworm live?
What does he see underground?
Can he hear us walking on the ground above?
What is his home like?
What does he eat?
What does he do for fun?

Write the answers to the questions on a sheet of chart paper. Then use the answers to help your children write a class story about earthworms. Print the completed story on a sheet of poster board. Ask a child to illustrate the poster and display it in the classroom.

The Magic Pebble

In *Sylvester And The Magic Pebble* by William Steig, Sylvester collects rocks. Read the story to your children. Then ask each child to name something she likes to collect. Print the child's name and the sentence, "I collect _____ [thing collected]," on a sheet of chart paper. Copy each sentence on a sheet of paper. Have each child illustrate her sentence. Then bind the papers together to create a class book titled "Things We Collect." Next divide the class into small groups and assign each group a day to bring in their collections for a show-and-tell activity.

Rock Words

Draw a large rock on a sheet of poster board. Cut out the rock shape and attach it to a wall in the classroom. Print the word *rock* in the center of the poster. Then ask your youngsters to name synonyms for *rock* such as *pebble, stone, boulder, cinder,* and *gravel.* Write each word on the poster as it is dictated.

The Pebble Found

Read aloud *Alexander And The Wind-Up Mouse* by Leo Lionni. Then let your children make a colorful cape—in colors similar to those on the lizard's body—in preparation for a follow-up activity. First cut out a cape from an old white sheet. Use a black permanent or fabric marker to divide the cape into sections. Let a small group of children use markers or fabric paint to color each section. Next tell each child to find a partner and sit in a circle on the floor. Have a pair of student volunteers stand. Ask one child to pretend to be the lizard. Let him wear the cape and hold a construction-paper moon. Ask the other child to pretend to be Alexander and to hold a purple pebble. Then instruct the two children to repeat the following dialogue:

    Alexander—"Lizard, lizard, in the bush."
    Lizard—"The moon is round, the pebble found. Who or what do you wish to be?"
    Alexander—"I want to be _____."
(Let the child fill in the blank.)

Have the lizard grant the wish, and ask Alexander to use appropriate sounds and body movements to imitate the animal. Then let another pair of children repeat the activity.

SCIENCE

Sand And Soil

Let each child pretend she is a geologist as she investigates the composition of sand and soil samples. Have a small group of children sit around a table. Place a tray of sand and a tray of soil in the center of the table. Give each child a magnifying glass and a copy of the reproducible on the bottom half of page 112. Instruct her to spread a thin layer of glue in the center of the circle labeled "Sand." Then let her sprinkle a small amount of sand on the glue. Have her count to thirty and shake off the excess into the sand tray. Tell her to follow the same procedure with the soil. Now she is ready to begin the investigation. Allow her a few minutes to observe the sand and soil samples through the magnifying glass. Then conclude by asking the following questions:

How does the sand feel? The soil?
What do you see in the sand? The soil?
What do you think the sand is made of? The soil?

Rock Talk

For homework, ask each child to bring in a rock collection. Let each child show his favorite rock to the class and describe it. Display the collections in the classroom and allow each child time during the week to observe them. One note: A cardboard egg carton makes an excellent container for carrying and displaying rocks.

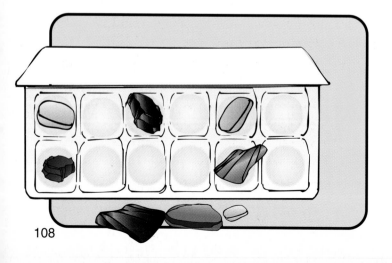

Rock Investigation

Ask each child to bring a rock to school to contribute to a class rock collection. Place the rocks in a large container in a learning center. Let each child in the center choose four or five rocks. Tell her to use a magnifying glass to look closely at each rock. Then give her a copy of the lab sheet at the top of page 113. Ask her to circle an answer for each question.

Worm Watching

Create an underground world for worm watching in the classroom. Cover the bottom of a glass jar with gravel. Mix equal amounts of dirt and dried leaves. Fill the jar half-full with the dirt-and-leaves mixture. Put four or five earthworms on top of the mixture. Place the jar in a cool place out of direct light. Add three teaspoons of water to the jar daily.

To extend the activity, place the jar in a closet. After a few days, take it out and observe the activity of the worms. Then leave the jar in a well-lit room for a few days. What changes occur? Finally lightly saturate the soil with water and watch what happens.

SOCIAL STUDIES

Community Workers

Invite a stonemason, stonecutter, geologist, or jeweler to talk with your class about his work with rocks. Ask him to bring in examples of the types of rocks he uses and describe them to your children.

Field Trip

If your school is located near a rock quarry, arrange a field trip to visit the facilities. If not, plan a visit to a science museum that includes a display of rocks.

Rock Hounds

Rocks and minerals are used in a variety of products such as paint, tires, automobile batteries, aluminum cans, detergent, plastic, bricks, glass, toothpaste, pencil points, and baby powder. Give each child a copy of the reproducible at the bottom of page 113. For homework, ask her to find out how many of the products listed are in her home. Ask her to circle an answer for each question.

If I Were A Rock

Rocks can be used to build a house, cover a dirt road, make beautiful jewelry, or create a unique statue. Ask each child to imagine he is a rock. Would he want to be part of a fireplace or a walkway? Or would he rather be a paperweight? Have each child draw a picture of what he would want to be if he were a rock, then write or dictate a sentence about his picture. Let each child share his picture with the others.

Rock Problems

Let small groups of children work cooperatively and brainstorm to solve the following problem. Then have each group dramatize or draw a picture of their solution.

Two friends have been collecting rocks on the playground. They have put the rocks together in a big pile. There are too many rocks to carry, and they are too heavy. How will the children get the rocks home?

ART

Sandpaper Prints

Have each child in a small group use crayons to color a design on a sheet of fine sandpaper. Then give her a sheet of white paper that is the same size as the sandpaper. Have her place the white paper on top of the sandpaper. Put newspaper under the sandpaper and over the white paper to protect your iron. With your youngsters safely out of reach, carefully press the paper with an electric iron set on low until the crayon shows through the white paper. Gently peel the white paper off the sandpaper. The resulting print will look as though it has been colored with dots.

Gravel Mosaic

To prepare for this activity, purchase three or four bags of different-colored aquarium gravel from a pet store. Pour each bag of gravel into a separate container. Then have each child in a learning center draw a simple design such as the outline of a fish or snake on a sheet of cardboard. Tell her to spread a thin layer of glue over one area of the design. Then have her sprinkle a small amount of gravel over the glue. Tell her to wait thirty seconds, shake off the excess gravel, and repeat the process with another area of the picture.

Textured Clay

Have each child in a learning center roll out a slab of clay with a rolling pin. Then let her use a variety of objects such as tiles, pinecones, shells, straws, plastic spoons, and kitchen utensils to create an interesting texture in the clay's surface. Insert a bent paper clip into the back of each slab and allow it to air-dry for several days.

Rock Diorama

Let each child choose two or three rocks from his collection (see "Rock Talk" on page 108) and use them in a rock diorama. Have him cut out scenic pictures of natural settings such as a forest, seashore, or streambed and glue them inside a shoebox. Then let him place the rocks and additional materials such as twigs and seashells in the shoebox to complete the setting.

SNACK

Dirt

Prepare a small package of chocolate Jell-O instant pudding according to package directions. Mix the pudding together with a thawed eight-ounce container of Cool Whip. Crush a sixteen-ounce package of Oreo cookies. Stir half the crushed cookies into the pudding mixture. Spoon the mixture into clear, plastic cups and top with remaining cookies. Refrigerate for one hour. Decorate with cake decorating flowers or Gummy worms.

CULMINATING ACTIVITY

Rock And Roll Party

Throw a rock and roll party—fifties' style. Ask your children to come dressed as fifties' rockers. Then let them dance to selected tunes from *Dancin' Magic* CD by Joanie Bartels or *All-Time Favorite Dances* CD from Kimbo.

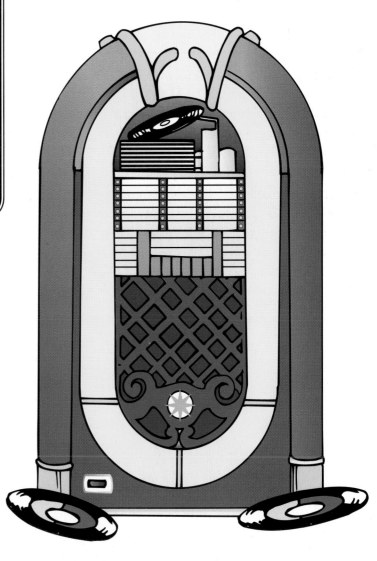

Rocks, Sand, And Soil

Use with "Heavy As A Rock" on page 104.

Rocks 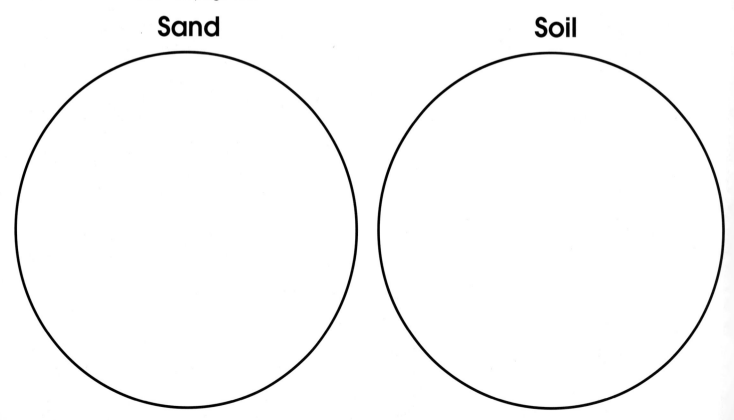	Number of counters

Use with "Sand And Soil" on page 108.

Sand   Soil

1. Did you find a rock that sparkles  ?   yes   no

2. Did you find a rock with stripes ?   yes   no

3. Did you find a rock that is smooth ?   yes   no

4. Did you find a rock with sharp points ?   yes   no

5. Did you find a rock with red in it ?   yes   no

- -

Use with "Rock Hounds" on page 109.

In your home, do you have...

      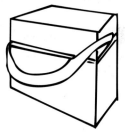

a can of paint?   baby powder?   laundry detergent?

yes   no   yes   no   yes   no

an aluminum can?   a set of glasses?   a tube of toothpaste?

yes   no   yes   no   yes   no

Recycling/Ecology

Reduce, reuse, and recycle—the three Rs for a healthy planet. These activities will teach your youngsters to reduce waste and use most things more than once.

MATH

Paper Wads

To prepare for this activity, make 25 small paper wads. Place the wads in the center of a table. Shuffle a deck of 1–50 number cards and place them in a stack face-down on the table. Assemble a small group of children around the table. Tell each child to draw one card from the deck. Then ask the group to decide who has the highest number. Let that child take a paper wad from the pile. Have each child place his card in a discard pile and resume play. Continue until all the number cards are gone. The child with the most paper wads at the end of the game is the winner. Shuffle the cards and play again using the lowest number. One note: Attach a number chart to the wall for easy reference by the children.

Plastic Lids

Ask each child to bring in several unwanted plastic lids from home. Place the lids in a large container. Then have a small group of children sort the lids into three containers labeled "small," "medium," and "large," respectively.

Newspaper Toss

Instruct each child in a learning center to crumple up sheets of newspaper to create ten paper balls. Have her place the balls in a plastic grocery bag. Then set a large paper bag on the floor. Ask each child to toss her newspaper balls, one at a time, into the paper bag. Have her tally the number of balls that land in the bag. Then tell her to put the balls back into the plastic bag and let another child have a turn. Instruct each child to total her score at the end of the activity. The child with the highest score is the winner.

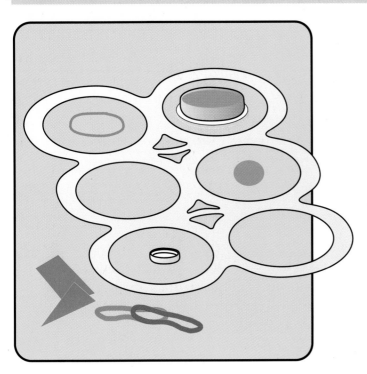

Six-Pack Math

Let your youngsters use six-pack beverage rings and other recyclable materials to make various sets. Place a container of small objects such as rubber bands, foam packing pieces, pom-poms, bread ties, lids, and paper scraps in a learning center. Give each child in the center a six-pack beverage ring. Have her use one attribute (such as things that are round or pom-poms that are red) to create a set inside the rings. Then let her tell why the objects belong in the set.

Milk Cap Math

Caps that come on plastic milk jugs make excellent manipulatives for patterning. If you do not have an ample supply on hand, ask parents to send some from home. Place the collected caps in a container. Then let a small group of children use them to make original patterns. Your youngsters can pattern using cap color, caps with or without writing, caps upside down and right-side up, and many other ways.

Scoop And Count

Place three empty laundry detergent boxes and their plastic scoops in a learning center. Fill each box with a different recyclable material such as broken crayons and paper wads. Tell each child in the center to fill a scoop with the materials from one box, then pour them onto a mat and count the number of objects. Have him repeat the procedure with the other materials. Let him tell you which set of objects had the most and which had the least number of items.

White Elephant Sale

A toy that is old and boring to one child can be new and exciting to another. Plan a white elephant sale for your children to buy and sell used toys. Send a note home to parents asking that each child bring in one or two small, inexpensive, used toy(s) for the sale. Also specify that the toys will not be returned. Price each toy and display it in the classroom. Then give each child play money. Let him use the money to purchase one or two toys from the sale. Your children will have fun while learning the value and usage of money.

LANGUAGE ARTS

Recycling Slogans

Brainstorm with your children a list of recycling slogans such as those listed below. Then give each child a piece of paper the size of a bumper sticker. Have her choose one of the slogans, copy it onto her paper strip, and then illustrate it. The bumper stickers can be attached to book bags, wagons, or bicycles. To vary the activity, let each child make a recycling bookmark. Give him a 2" x 6 1/2" strip of tagboard and let him print a slogan on it. Laminate the bookmarks for durability.

Protect Our Planet
Recycle Today!
Clean And Green
Recycler On Board
Going Green

Recyclables

Tell your children to sit in a circle on the floor. Give one child an empty liter bottle. Ask him to name one thing that could be made from the bottle. Then have him pass it to the next child and ask him to name something else. Continue the activity until a child gets stumped. Give that child another recyclable such as a newspaper or a milk jug, and repeat the procedure.

Yesterday's Stuff

Read the poem "Yesterday's Paper" by Mabel Watts, from *Read-Aloud Rhymes For The Very Young* selected by Jack Prelutsky. Then let your children make a class book titled "Yesterday's Stuff." Have each child think of one recyclable and dictate a sentence about it using the following format: "Yesterday's _____ makes a _____." Print the sentence on a sheet of paper and ask him to illustrate it. Bind the pages together inside a bright-colored cover.

Letter And Sound Sheet

Recycle an old sheet and make a fun game for your youngsters, too! Use fabric paint to paint the letters of the alphabet in random order on a solid-colored sheet. (Make sure the letters are large enough for a child to stand on.) Then place a set of alphabet cards in an empty shoebox and several recyclable tokens such as bottle caps in another. Spread the sheet on the floor and ask the children in a small group to stand around it. Give each child a plastic grocery bag. Tell one child to draw a card from the letter box, stand on the letter, and name a word that begins with the sound the letter makes. If he is correct, he may take a token from the token box and place it in his bag. If he is incorrect, another child gets a turn. At the end of the game, the child with the most tokens is the winner.

Trees Are Nice

Trees and other plants help our ecology by producing the oxygen that people and animals need to breathe. Read *A Tree Is Nice* by Janice May Udry and discuss other ways trees are important. List all of the ideas on a sheet of chart paper. Next give each child a leaf cutout. Have him copy one of the ways trees are used on the cutout. Then paint a tree trunk on the background paper of a bulletin board. Label the bulletin board "A Tree Is Nice" and attach the leaves to the tree trunk.

Keeping Clean And Green

Discuss with your children the importance of keeping the earth clean and green. Then ask them to think of things they could do to help keep the air, water, and land clean. List each idea on a sheet of chart paper. Next give each child a copy of the reproducible on page 122. Have her draw a picture of something she can do to keep the air, water, and land clean. Display the pictures on a bulletin board in the classroom or bind them together to create a class book.

Boxes And Sticks

Print the poem "Johnny" by Marci Ridlon, from *Read-Aloud Rhymes For The Very Young* selected by Jack Prelutsky, on a sheet of chart paper. Use the chart to help teach the poem to your children. Then print the name of each item that Johnny made from a box or a stick on a separate word card. Place the chart and word cards in a learning center. Have the children in the center attach the word cards over the matching words on the chart. Then ask the children to take turns reading the poem.

SCIENCE

Rot Pots

Help your children understand that all garbage does not disappear once it is thrown away. Fill five baby food jars half-full with soil. Add a different item to each jar such as a vegetable, toothpicks, crumpled scraps of newspaper, a plastic toy, and paper clips. Cover the items with additional soil. Then sprinkle the soil with water to keep it moist. Secure the lids on the jars and label each one. Then let your children observe the changes that occur (and do not occur) in the items over the next two weeks.

Noise Pollution

After discussing the different things that can pollute the air, water, and land, try this simple experiment to show your children how noise can pollute. Play a record and have your youngsters, one after another, begin making noises by clapping their hands, stomping their feet, or tapping their desks. Eventually the noises will make the record impossible to enjoy. Tell or signal to your children to stop their noisemaking. Then ask them to describe how noise can pollute. Finally discuss and list ways noises can pollute the school (children talking, running, and laughing) and home (dishwashers running, dogs barking, and babies crying).

Something Old, Something New

Stimulate creativity and help keep the earth clean and green with this homework assignment. Show your youngsters examples of how something old has been recycled into something new. For instance, you might show them a patchwork quilt that has been made from old fabric squares, a juice carton that has been made into a birdhouse, or an egg carton that has been recycled into seed pots. Next encourage each child to use her imagination to create something new from something old for a homework assignment. Let each child share her recycled item with the class. Then display the items in the classroom, media center, or school showcase.

SOCIAL STUDIES

Recycle At School

Begin a recycling program in your classroom by saving and reusing paper that is partially used. Label three grocery bags "Colored Paper Scraps," "One Side Only," and "Scratch Paper," respectively. Place the bags in a designated area of the classroom labeled "Recycling Center." Then ask your children to place their used papers in the designated bags instead of throwing them in the trash. Use the paper for art projects and note taking.

Recycling At Home

For homework, give each child a copy of the reproducible on page 123. Tell him to check off the items in his home that could be recycled. Then have him draw pictures of two additional items in his home that are also recyclable.

Litter Patrol

Each day of this unit, have your class patrol a different area on school grounds for litter. Before beginning the patrol, divide the class into groups. Give each group a wastebasket that has been decorated with recycling symbols. Discuss safety precautions in handling glass or metal. After the cleanup, ask each group to empty the litter into a large trash bag and throw it into the school dumpster. Finally let your children wash their hands and praise them for keeping the earth clean and green. To extend the activity, continue the patrol once a week during the school year and challenge other classes to get involved.

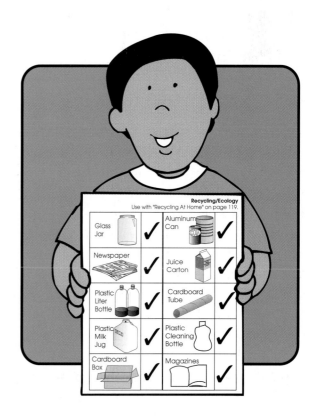

Invite An Expert

Your town or community is served by a waste management department or company. Arrange a time when a representative from the facility can visit your classroom and discuss the importance of recycling.

ART

Recycled Works Of Art

Ask your children to bring in items that can be recycled such as cardboard tubes, bread ties, newspapers, and shoeboxes. Place the items, glue, and masking tape in a learning center. Let each child in the center select a few of the items and create a sculpture by taping and/or gluing the pieces together.

Bottle People

Let each child in a small group create a unique bottle person with an empty plastic bottle, sand, newspaper sheets and strips, masking tape, liquid wallpaper paste, paint, paintbrushes, yarn, glue, ribbon, decorative fabric, and clear gloss enamel spray. To make a bottle person, partially fill a bottle with sand to help the bottle stand erect. Then wad two sheets of newspaper together into a tight ball to make the head. Pull a piece of the newspaper out from the ball to shape the neck. Insert the neck into the bottle's opening. Use masking tape to secure the head to the bottle. Cover the head, neck, and bottle with newspaper strips dipped in liquid wallpaper paste. Allow the paper strips to dry completely. Paint features on the head and colorful designs on the body. Attach yarn to the top of the head to make the hair. Add decorative materials such as fabric scraps and ribbon to the body. Then spray each bottle person with clear gloss enamel and let it dry.

Printing With Recyclables

To prepare for this activity, make printing blocks by cutting several squares from a corrugated cardboard box. Then glue a different recyclable material to each square. Materials may include shapes cut from sponges, cord or string, paper wads, or pieces of cardboard. Place the printing blocks, paintbrushes, tempera paint, and large sheets of paper in a learning center. Ask each child to choose a printing block and paint a thick coat of paint over the recyclable material. Then tell him to press the printing block on a sheet of paper to create an interesting design. Have him repeat the process until the paper is covered. When the paper is dry, use it as wrapping paper or a book cover, or mount it on a larger sheet of paper and display it in the classroom.

SNACK

Earth Cookies

Divide a can of white frosting in half. Color one-half of the frosting with blue food coloring and the other half with green. Then give each child a large sugar cookie on a napkin. Have him use a plastic knife or craft stick to spread the frosting on the cookie. Tell him to use the green for the land and the blue for the water to make his cookie resemble the earth.

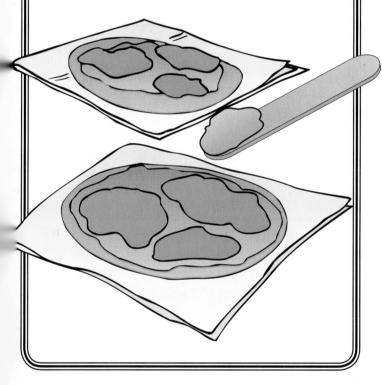

CULMINATING ACTIVITY

Earth Gifts

Ask each child to wear something blue and something green on the last day of the unit. Then let each child make a gift for the earth. Give him a green sheet of construction paper. Tell him to write a sentence or draw a picture on the paper of something he can do to keep the earth clean and green. Have him roll it up and tie a blue ribbon around it. Next let your children help you plant a tree or shrub on the school grounds. Afterwards ask each child to place his "gift" around the tree's trunk.

Air

Water

Land

Glass Jar		Aluminum Can	
Newspaper		Juice Carton	
Plastic Liter Bottle		Cardboard Tube	
Plastic Milk Jug			
Cardboard Box			

Over In The Meadow

Acquaint your children with the animals at the forest's edge as you stretch their awareness with these fun-to-do meadow activities.

MATH

Meadow Math

Create a meadow scene on a bulletin board in the classroom. Begin by covering the board with green paper. Use blue paper to make a pond and mount it on the green background. Complete the scene by adding flowers and sprigs of grass made from paper scraps. Make several bunny, butterfly, turtle, and fish cutouts. Each day, mount a different number of animals on the bulletin board. Ask your children questions similar to those listed below.

How many fish do you see?
How many fish were in the pond yesterday?
How many bunnies do you see?
Are there more bunnies than fish? How many more?

Then give each child a copy of the reproducible on page 132. Have him graph the number of animals on the board.

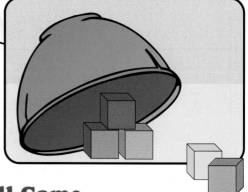

Shell Game

Tell a small group of children to sit around a table. Give each child a large container. Ask her to pretend it is a turtle's shell. Then give her five small blocks. Tell her to put the shell on top of the blocks to cover them. Then have her take two blocks from under the shell and place them beside the shell. Ask her to tell how many blocks are under the shell now. Have her lift the shell to check her answer. Continue the activity in the same manner, asking each child to place different combinations of blocks underneath and beside the shell.

Ordering Earthworms

Cut a quantity of different lengths of cord or brown ribbon. Place the pieces of cord in a container and label it "Earthworms." Tell each child in a small group to take five "earthworms" from the container and place them on a mat in order from the shortest to the longest. Afterwards, have him place them back into the container and repeat the process with five more pieces of cord.

Greater Than/Less Than

Give each child a copy of the reproducible on page 133. Tell her to write a numeral that is less than each set of meadow animals in the less-than column and a numeral that is greater than each set in the greater-than column. To vary the activity for younger children, ask them to draw an appropriate number of meadow animals in each column.

How Many Babies?

How many baby animals are in the book *Over In The Meadow* illustrated by Ezra Jack Keats? Read the poem to your children. Then let each child estimate how many babies are in the meadow. Ask him to write his estimation on a slip of paper. Read the poem again, stopping after each verse to tally the number of babies. At the conclusion of the story, total the number of tally marks. Then ask each child to compare his estimation with the total to determine who came the closest.

Leapfrog

Use the game of Leapfrog to reinforce the position words *beside*, *behind*, *between*, and *front*. Ask several student volunteers to position themselves as frogs ready to leap. Direct one child to leap beside a second child. Tell a third child to leap behind another. Continue the game in the same fashion until each word has been illustrated. Then divide the class into small groups. Have your children listen to your directions and play Leapfrog in groups. To vary the activity, play Leapfrog using ordinal position words.

LANGUAGE ARTS

"Little White Duck"

Let your children listen to "Little White Duck" by Raffi from the CD *Everything Grows.* Next ask four volunteers to act out the song while you play it again. Then give each child a copy of the reproducible on page 132. Have him cut apart the pictures and paste them on a sheet of construction paper in the proper sequence in which they appear in the song.

Busy Beavers

Read the book *Busy Beavers* by Lydia Dabcovich. Then list the sound words *crunch, plop, splash,* and *thump,* which name sounds made by the beavers in the story. Discuss the action which creates each of the sounds. Then have your children think of other ways these sounds can be made. Next write each of the four words on an individual index card. Place the index cards, paper, pencils, and crayons in a writing center. Tell the children in the center to copy each word on a separate sheet of paper and draw a picture of something that might create that sound. Bind each child's four pages together inside a bright-colored cover to make an individual book titled "Sound Words."

Animal ABC Order

Have older students try this activity to reinforce alphabetizing. Print each of the following meadow animal names on individual word cards: *ant, beaver, chipmunk, deer, earthworm, frog, grasshopper, katydid, lizard, mouse, owl, rabbit, snail, turtle,* and *wasp.* Place the word cards in a learning center. Ask the children in the center to put the names in alphabetical order.

"The Frog On The Log"

Your children will enjoy the repetitive rhythm of the delightful "The Frog On The Log" by Ilo Orleans from *Read-Aloud Rhymes For The Very Young* selected by Jack Prelutsky. Print the poem on a sheet of chart paper. Use the chart to teach the poem to your children. Then divide the class into six groups. Assign each group one stanza of the poem and guide them in reading it chorally as a poem.

Waddle Or Wiggle?

Waddle, wiggle, slither, hop, crawl—your children can do them all! But what about a lizard or a duck? Make a list of meadow animals on a sheet of chart paper. Then have your children think of one word to describe how each animal moves. Print the movement word beside each animal's name. Let each child choose a word pair from the chart paper. Have her copy the words on a sheet of paper and draw a picture to illustrate them. Bind the pages together to create a class book titled "Waddle Or Wiggle?"

Reading Fun

Read the book *If You Give A Mouse A Cookie* by Laura Joffe Numeroff. Then review the story and make a list of each item asked for by the mouse. For the following day, gather an example of each item on the list. Place the items in random order on the floor and ask your children to sit in a circle around them. Reread the book, stopping to ask your youngsters what the mouse will ask for next. Let your children place the items in sequential order as they are named.

City		Country
apartment		house
townhouse		farm
house		ranch
car		truck
taxi		tractor
subway		horse
tuxedo		jeans
suit		overalls
dress		straw hat
fast foods		fresh fruit
		milk
		vegetables

Opposite Mice

Read aloud "City Mouse—Country Mouse" from *City Mouse—Country Mouse And Two More Mouse Tales From Aesop* illustrated by John Wallner. Ask your children to listen for opposites in the text and look for opposites in the illustrations as you read. Then write the words "City" and "Country" at the top of a sheet of chart paper. Let your youngsters help you list the different types of housing, food, clothing, transportation, and animals found in the city and in the country. Afterwards ask each child if he would rather be a city mouse or a country mouse, and have him explain why.

Act It Out

The descriptive language used in *The Snail's Spell* by Joanne Ryder makes it an excellent book for dramatic play. Read the book aloud to your class. Then reread it and ask each child to pretend to be the snail and act out the story.

SCIENCE

Camouflage

Many meadow animals—such as toads, lizards, and rabbits—match the color of their surroundings to help them hide from their enemies. Tell your children that the term for this special ability is *camouflage*. Then let your youngsters participate in a camouflage game. To prepare for the game, cut several strips of matching construction paper, wrapping paper, and/or wallpaper. Tape some of the strips to objects that are different colors and others to objects that are the same color. Show your children an example of a paper strip they are to find. Then let them look around the room. Each time a strip is found, attach it to a sheet of poster board. Once all the strips have been located, discuss why some were easier to find than others.

Beaver Dam

Help your students create a model of a beaver dam. First cut a hole in the center of a heavy sheet of cardboard. Then paint the cardboard blue to resemble water and let it dry. To make the beaver lodge, place a large bowl upside down over the hole. Cover the bowl with a layer of clay. Press small sticks and twigs into the clay. Next read aloud *Busy Beavers* by Lydia Dabcovich. Afterwards let small groups of children take turns reenacting the story using stick puppets and the beaver dam model.

Classroom Critters

Most children are familiar with the small mammals often kept as classroom pets such as gerbils, mice, guinea pigs, and hamsters. During this unit, introduce your children to other classroom critters such as snails, crickets, grasshoppers, earthworms, turtles, and frogs. These animals can be found in pet stores, bait shops, or your own backyard. They require little care and can be returned to their natural environment once you are finished with them.

How Animals Move

Print the words "crawl," "walk," "swim," and "fly" at the top of individual sheets of poster board. Ask your youngsters to name animals that move in one of the four ways. Then have them cut out pictures of animals from nature magazines and attach them to the appropriate posters.

SOCIAL STUDIES

Fears

Everyone is afraid of something. In the book *Franklin In The Dark* by Paulette Bourgeois, Franklin, a turtle, will not go into his shell because he is afraid of the dark. Read the story aloud to your youngsters. Then have them name the other animals in the book and their fears. Next have the children describe what each animal does to overcome its fear. Conclude the discussion by asking each child to name something that frightens him. Encourage your children to think of ways to help each other overcome their fears.

Field Trip

Plan a field trip to a state or national park, and take your youngsters on a nature hunt for small meadow animals and their homes. Then enjoy a picnic lunch before you return to school. If your school is not located near a park, invite a park ranger to visit your classroom and discuss her work with animals.

Who Lives Here?

Each type of meadow animal lives in the home that best meets its needs. Read aloud *If You Walk Down This Road* by Kate Duke. Then discuss the different homes of the various animals in the book. Next show your youngsters photographs of animal homes from factual books and describe the features that make them unique. Then play Who Lives Here? To play this game, describe an animal home and ask your children to name the animal that lives there.

Rules

Peter Rabbit's mother told him not to go into Mr. McGregor's garden. But Peter disobeyed his mother and got into a lot of trouble. Read aloud *The Tale Of Peter Rabbit* by Beatrix Potter. Then discuss why rules are important. Have your children help you list several safety rules such as "Never play with matches," "Don't talk to strangers," and "Look both ways before crossing the street." Then ask them to describe what could happen if each of the rules was not obeyed.

ART

Meadow Animals

Have your children follow these simple, step-by-step directions to draw meadow animals.

Baby Birds In A Nest
1. Draw a half-circle.
2. Draw three small circles on top of the half-circle.
3. Add an eye and a beak to each circle.

Duck In A Pond
1. Draw an oval.
2. Draw a small circle on top of the oval.
3. Add an eye, a beak, and a tail.
4. Make wavy lines for the water.

Turtle
1. Draw a half-circle.
2. Draw a small circle on the end of the half-circle.
3. Add an eye, a tail, and legs.

Fish Puppets

Have each child trace around his hand on a piece of tagboard; then cut it out. Let him use markers or paints to decorate the cutout to resemble a fish. Then attach a tongue depressor to the back to create a fish puppet. Play "I Caught A Fish" from the cassette *Wee Sing And Play* by Pamela Conn Beall and Susan Hagen Nipp, and let your children use their puppets to act out the poem.

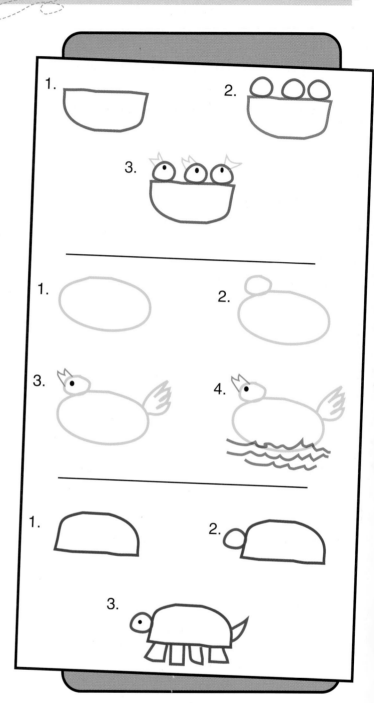

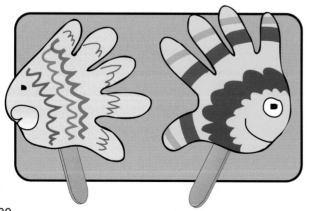

Torn-Paper Turtle

Let each child in a small group use a pattern to trace a turtle shape on a sheet of green or brown construction paper. Have him cut out the turtle. Then glue bright-colored pieces of torn paper on its back to make a decorative shell.

SNACK

Owl Eyes

Freeze a tube of slice-and-bake sugar cookie dough for one hour. Remove the wrapper and slice the frozen dough into 1/4-inch slices. Give each child in a small group two slices. Have her overlap them slightly on an ungreased cookie sheet. Press the two slices together. Then push a chocolate chip into the center of each slice of dough to create the eyes. Bake at 350° for 12 minutes. Then, press a candy corn between the eyes to make the beak.

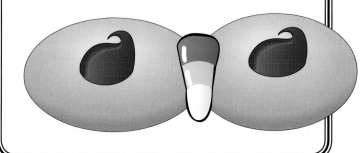

CULMINATING ACTIVITY

Meadow Mural

Have your children work together to create an attractive meadow mural. Cover a bulletin board with white paper. Draw a meadow scene on the paper. Include trees, grass, a pond, the sun, logs, and rocks. Then let small groups of children take turns painting the scene. Ask other small groups to use construction-paper scraps, markers, and crayons to make the meadow animals. Attach the animals to the scene to complete the mural.

Over In The Meadow
Bar Graph
Use with "Meadow Math" on page 124.

Sequence Cards
Use with " 'Little White Duck' " on page 126.

1	2	3	4

Less		More

Insects And Spiders

Adjust your safari hat and binoculars as you embark on an insect and spider adventure. Observations of these creatures will open doors for your youngsters' increased knowledge and wonder about insects and spiders.

MATH

Bugs In A Jar

Place several plastic bugs in a clear glass jar. Then write the correct number of bugs in the jar and two other random numbers (perhaps one number greater than and one less than the actual number) on a piece of folded poster board. Place the bug jar, poster board, scraps of paper, a pencil, and another glass jar on a table in the classroom. Ask each child to estimate how many bugs are in the jar. Tell them the correct number is one of the three numbers printed on the poster board. Have each child write his name and estimation on a slip of paper and place it in the empty jar. After every child has had a turn, tell the class the actual number of bugs that are in the jar. Then pull out the slips and compare how many children chose each of the three numbers. Finally repeat the activity, placing a different number of bugs in the jar and making a different poster each day of the unit.

"The Ants Go Marching"

Lead your class in singing "The Ants Go Marching…" from *And The Green Grass Grew All Around: Folk Poetry From Everyone* by Alvin Schwartz. Then give each child ten raisins. Tell her to pretend the raisins are ants. Ask the following subtraction questions and have her use the raisins to help find the answers:

If there are 10 ants and 2 march down into the ground, how many are left? *(8)*

If 1 more ant marches down into the ground, how many are left? *(7)*

If 2 more ants march down into the ground, how many are left? *(5)*

If 4 more ants march down into the ground, how many are left? *(1)*

If 1 more ant marches down into the ground, how many are left? *(0)*

"I Hate Bugs! I Like Them."

Read the poem "I Hate Bugs! I Like Them," from *Bugs* by Mary Ann Hoberman. Then ask your children to help you list the bugs named in the poem. Ask each child to choose one bug from the list and copy it onto his paper. Have him draw a picture of it using his imagination and basic knowledge of the bug. Finally graph the bug drawings to see which ones were drawn the most, the least, and not at all.

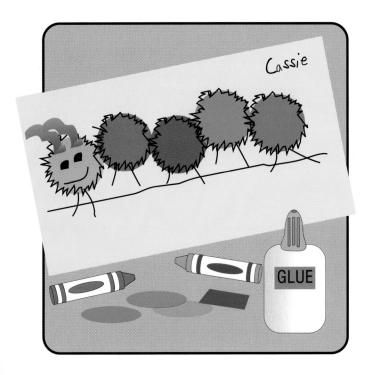

Caterpillars

Give each child a sheet of yellow construction paper, glue, and five different-colored circles cut from orange, red, purple, green, and blue construction paper. Tell her to follow your directions for making a colorful caterpillar. On the yellow construction paper, have her glue the orange circle on first, the red circle second, the purple circle third, and so on. Then let her use crayons or paper scraps to add features to the caterpillar. Afterwards, ask her to name the ordinal position of each circle.

How Many Bugs?

Prepare a counting book of bugs for each child. Insert five blank pages inside a bright-colored cover and print the title "How Many Bugs?" on the front. Place the books, markers, a stamp pad, and rubber insect stamps and spider stamps in a learning center. Instruct each child to print a number between one and twenty on each of the five pages. Then have him use the rubber stamps and the stamp pad to print the corresponding number of bugs on each page. One note: If insect and spider rubber stamps are unavailable, let each child create bugs using his fingerprints and a fine-line marker.

Ladybug Addition

Have a small group of children sit around a table. Place a set of dominoes (removing the zero, eleven and twelve domino) facedown in the center of the table. Then give each child a copy of one of the four playing cards on page 142. Tell a child to turn over one domino. If the number of dots on the domino totals a number on her playing card, have her place the domino over the number. If not, tell her to return the domino facedown on the table. Continue play with another child. The game ends when one child covers her entire playing card with dominoes.

Spider Legs

An insect has six legs. How many legs does a spider have? Eight! Have a small group of children sit around a table. Give each child a black, four-inch circle to represent a spider's body. Place a number cube and a quantity of clothespins to represent spider legs in the center of the table. In turn, have each child roll the number cube. The child who rolls the highest number may clip one clothespin to her circle. The first child to attach all eight legs to her spider is the winner. To vary the activity, play the game using the lowest number rolled each turn.

LANGUAGE ARTS

Buggy Syllables

Print each of the following words on individual cards. Place the cards in a safari hat. Let each child draw one card from the hat. Read the word on the card. Ask the child to tell if the word has one, two, or three syllables. Then place the word card in one of three pockets on a pocket chart according to the number of syllables. To vary the activity, tell your children to listen to the number of times you clap your hands as you say each word. Then have them hold up the appropriate number of fingers to indicate the number of syllables.

ant	cricket	grasshopper
tick	firefly	butterfly
moth	stinkbug	ladybug
fly	beetle	dragonfly
wasp	hornet	mosquito
flea	termite	bumblebee
roach	mayfly	katydid

Old Black Fly

The ABC book, *Old Black Fly* by Jim Aylesworth, describes the many things an old black fly did one day. Each of the twenty-six events highlights a different letter of the alphabet. Read the story to your children for enjoyment. Then reread the story, stopping after each event to let your children name the words that begin with the particular letter. Print the words on a sheet of chart paper. Then copy them on index cards and illustrate each card. Place the index cards in a learning center, along with blank index cards. Have the children in the center use the word cards to copy the words onto the blank cards.

Guess Who

To prepare for this activity, attach five pictures of different insects to individual index cards. Print the name of each insect under its picture. Then place the cards inside a bug box or safari hat. Each day, let a student volunteer draw a card from the box. Tell him to describe the insect to the class without naming it. Encourage the child to use words detailing the insect's colors, size, wings, antennae, eyes, and other interesting features. As the volunteer describes the insect, have each child use crayons to draw a picture of it on a sheet of paper. When the description and drawings are complete, let the children guess the name of the insect. Repeat the activity each day of the unit.

Wasps

Print the poem "Wasps" by Dorothy Aldis, from *The Random House Book Of Poetry For Children* selected by Jack Prelutsky, on a sheet of chart paper. Use the chart to teach the poem to your youngsters. Then cut out a picture of each thing a wasp likes, such as coffee, syrup, tea, soda, and butter. Glue the pictures on index cards and laminate for durability. Attach a small mirror or a piece of aluminum foil to another index card to represent the word *me*. Then place the picture cards, the mirror card, and the chart in a learning center. Tell the children in the center to attach the cards to the chart beside the appropriate words and read the poem aloud.

Ants

Two Bad Ants by Chris Van Allsburg describes a day in the life of two mischievous ants from their perspective. As you read the book to your children, have them name the strange objects encountered by the ants such as "the crystals"; "the giant scoop"; "the hot, brown liquid"; and "the cave." Then ask your children to guess what the ants might call other objects such as a fork, a napkin, and a bar of soap.

Honeybee Hive

Acquaint your children with the contractions *can't, won't, don't, she'll, he'll, we'll, you've, we've,* and *I've.* Then print each one on the body of a honeybee cutout. Next staple a large hive cutout to a bulletin board. Print the two words that make up each contraction on the hive. Attach the honeybees around the hive in random order. Each day let your children make up sentences using the contractions. At the end of the week, let the honeybees fly to their hive, and attach each one over the two words it represents. To vary the activity, print lowercase letters on the bee cutouts and corresponding uppercase letters on the hive.

Be A Butterfly

Where Butterflies Grow by Joanne Ryder is a beautifully illustrated book about the life cycle of a butterfly. Read the book aloud to your children. Then discuss the various stages a caterpillar goes through before becoming a butterfly. Reread the book and let your youngsters act out each event. Begin by asking each child to curl up in a ball to represent the egg and turning off the lights until the caterpillar crawls out into the brightness. Continue the activity until the butterfly emerges from the chrysalis and flies away to look for butterflies like himself.

The Very Hungry Caterpillar

At the beginning of the week, read *The Very Hungry Caterpillar* by Eric Carle. Afterwards have your children name the different things eaten by the caterpillar. Then give each child a sheet of paper with the sentence, "On Monday I ate _____," printed at the bottom. Ask her to draw a picture of one thing she ate for breakfast or lunch above the sentence. Print the name of the food in the blank. Repeat the activity each day of the unit. Then staple the pages together to create an individual book titled "The Very Hungry Girl" or "The Very Hungry Boy." To extend the activity, let each child complete the Saturday and Sunday pages for homework before binding the pages together.

The Old Lady Who Swallowed A Fly

Read *There Was An Old Lady Who Swallowed A Fly* illustrated by Pam Adams. Then collect a stuffed toy or picture representative of each animal in the book. Next paint a picture of the old lady's head on a sheet of poster board. Cut it out and cut a large opening for her mouth. Attach the cutout to a clean wastebasket. Then give each child in a small group one of the stuffed animals or pictures. Reread the story and let the youngsters put the animals in the old lady's mouth as they are named.

SCIENCE

Insects

Read the poem "Every Insect" by Dorothy Aldis, from *Animals, Animals* by Eric Carle. Then show your children a large picture of an insect. Point out the six legs, the three body parts (*head*, *thorax*, and *abdomen*), and the antennae. Then give each child a copy of the insect reproducible on page 143. Tell her to color the picture, cut around the solid black lines, and glue the three sections to a sheet of construction paper in the correct order.

Helpful And Harmful Insects

Helpful insects include butterflies, moths, wasps, bees, and others that pollinate flowering plants. These insects also pollinate plants that produce fruits and vegetables such as apples, oranges, and cotton. Ladybugs help farmers by eating harmful insects that destroy crops. Silkworms are important because they make the silk we use in clothing such as ties and scarfs. Honeybees produce honey and beeswax. Helpful insects keep the environment clean by eating the remains of dead plants and animals. They are also a source of food for animals such as frogs, fish, and birds.

Harmful insects include the boll weevil which damages cotton, the corn ear worm which attacks corn, the Japanese beetle which eats the leaves and fruits of plants, and the Hessian fly which destroys wheat. Other harmful insects can destroy items in our homes. For example, clothes moths and carpet beetles eat holes in things made of fabric or fur; silverfish ruin books; termites destroy wooden beams and flooring; and cockroaches, ants, and flies spoil food. Insects such as biting flies and mosquitoes inject a poison into our skin that causes itching and soreness.

Share these facts with your children; then set up a science center in the classroom where children can identify helpful and harmful insects. Include factual books, pictures, insects in clear plastic containers, and examples of things harmful insects have damaged.

138

Spiders

Spiders are not insects. Show your children a large picture of a spider and ask them to tell why. (Spiders have eight legs, two body parts, and no wings or antennae.) Next give each child a copy of the spider reproducible on page 143. Have him color the picture, cut around the solid black lines, and glue the sections to a sheet of construction paper in the correct order.

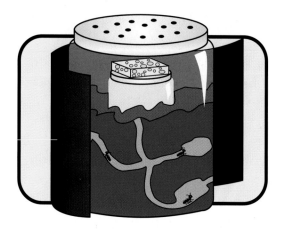

Build An Ant Colony

Help students observe the fascinating world of ants by building a classroom ant colony. (Discourage students from collecting ants at home, as many ants bite.) Follow these steps; then have students record their observations in their science journals.

1. Place a small jar (with the lid screwed on) inside a large, lidded jar.
2. Poke very small holes (smaller than an ant) in the large jar's lid.
3. Find an ant hill or a place with loose soil. Use a small shovel to gently dig up the ants and soil. Be sure that you include a queen in your colony. The queen ant is larger than the other ants.
4. Put the soil and ants in the large jar in the space surrounding the smaller jar.
5. Cover the jar with black paper so that the ants will tunnel close to the glass. Remove the paper only during observation periods.
6. Show students how to feed the ants periodically with very small bread crumbs, birdseed, or other small pieces of food. Place a damp sponge on top of the small jar. Be sure to keep the sponge damp at all times.
7. Have students observe the ants often and answer questions such as the following:
   • How do the ants spend their time?
   • Do the ants seem to communicate with each other? How?
   • How do ants carry food?

SOCIAL STUDIES

Insect Jobs

Social insects, such as all ants, many bees, and all termites, live in organized communities in which members have specialized jobs. For example, the *queen* in these colonies lays the eggs. The *workers* have many different tasks. Some care for the young. Others guard and defend the colony. Others clean and enlarge the nest, and some search for food. Discuss the jobs of social insects with your children. Then discuss various jobs of workers within the school such as the principal, teacher, custodian, nurse, secretary, librarian or media specialist, and cafeteria worker. Ask the children to describe each person's job. Then invite each of these people to visit your classroom and talk about his or her duties and responsibilities.

Pest Control Expert

Invite a pest control expert to visit your classroom. Ask him to bring examples of harmful insects and some of the items they have damaged. Also have him describe the methods he uses to control insects.

PLAN AHEAD

Food	Clothes	Shelter	Heat	Money
canning	storing seasonal clothes	add insulation	wood	savings account
freezing				budget

Plan Ahead

Read aloud "The Grasshopper And The Ant" from *Aesop's Fables* retold by Anne Terry White. Discuss how the hardworking ant worked all summer to save food for the winter and the lazy grasshopper only hopped, leaped, and sang. Then talk about ways we prepare for the future such as freezing and canning food, saving money in the bank, and storing seasonal clothes.

Beekeeper

Invite a beekeeper to visit your classroom. Ask him to bring his smoker, hive tools, and special clothing he wears to protect himself from stings. Have him describe the various parts of the hive, then discuss the method he uses for extracting honey from it.

ART

Hairy Spider

Use a fine-line marker to draw the outline of a spider on a sheet of paper. Make several copies of the outline on fluorescent paper. Ask a small group of children to sit around a table. Give each child a copy of the spider and a sheet of black construction paper. Tell him to tear the black paper into very small pieces. Have him glue the paper pieces in the center of the circle and on the legs to create a hairy spider. Then let him glue eight small pieces of red construction paper to the spider's head to create the eyes. Cut around the spider, leaving a border of fluorescent paper around the edge. Attach the completed spiders to a bulletin board or a string web.

Bug Or Spider Hats

Let each child create a hat representative of her favorite insect or spider. Cut a wide strip of paper to fit around her head. Then let her use markers, paint, and paper scraps to decorate the strip. Encourage her to include features such as eyes, antennae, and wings (for an insect) or eyes (for a spider) on the hat. Next have her fan-fold thin strips of paper to create the legs (six for an insect or eight for a spider). Staple the legs to the hat. Then staple the hat together so it fits the child's head.

Bug Box

Give each child a round oatmeal box and a sheet of construction paper. Let him use paint or markers to decorate the paper. Then tell him to glue the paper around the outside of the oatmeal box. Cut a hole in the side of the box. Cover the hole with a piece of cellophane. Use a knife to cut slits in the lid. Attach a yarn handle to the lid and place it on the oatmeal box. Then take your youngsters on a hunt for insects they can place in their bug boxes.

Butterfly

Let each child create a colorful butterfly with a sheet of construction paper, tempera paint, and plastic spoons. Fold the sheets of paper in half and give one to each child in a small group. Tell her to unfold the paper and to spoon drops of tempera paint on the paper, mainly along the fold line. Then refold the paper and have her rub it with the palm of her hand, from the fold to the edge of the paper. Open the paper. If more color is needed, add drops of tempera paint to the paper and repeat the procedure. Open the paper and let the paint dry. Then refold the paper and cut it into the shape of a butterfly. Mount the butterflies on construction paper or attach them to a bulletin board.

SNACK

Spider Cookies

Give each child two sandwich cookies. Have her insert eight pieces of string licorice into the cream of one cookie to create the spider's legs. Next tell her to place the cookies side by side. Let her use a plastic knife to spread canned frosting on both cookies. Then tell her to place eight mini chocolate chips on the cookie with the legs to create the spider eyes.

CULMINATING ACTIVITY

Butterfly Garden

Select an area on the school grounds suitable for a flower garden. Let your children plant a variety of fragrant flowers that attract butterflies such as creeping phlox, primroses, candytuft, purple or crimson aubrieta, yellow alyssum, bluebells, sweet rocket, scabiosa, and thistles.

Insects And Spiders Playing Cards
Use with "Ladybug Addition" on page 135.

2 🐞	5 🐞
🐞 8	🐞 1
9 🐞	10 🐞
🐞 6	🐞 4
🐞 4	8 🐞
7 🐞	🐞 2
🐞 9	6 🐞
5 🐞	🐞 3

Use with "Insects" on page 138.

Use with "Spiders" on page 138.

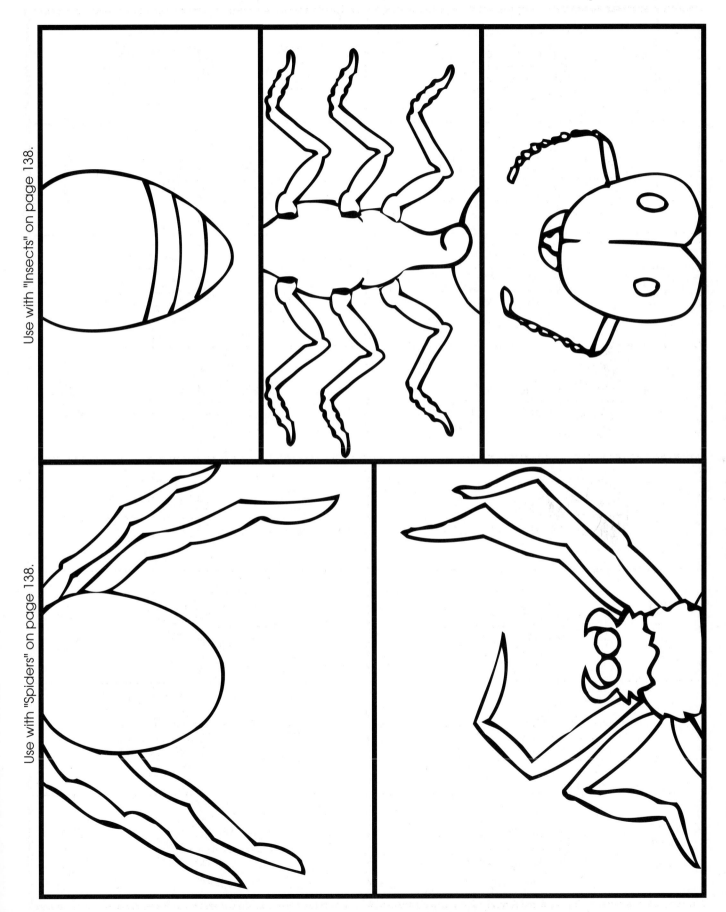

School's Out

I'm bored! There's nothing to do! These activities will ensure that your children never utter these words during the summer months. Review popular games, stories, songs, and poems, and teach your children new ones that will encourage learning over their vacation.

MATH

Checkers Game

This modified game of checkers will provide your youngsters with an opportunity to exercise thinking skills. Have a small group of children sit around a table. Divide the group into pairs. Place six checkers on the table between each pair. Tell the partners to take turns removing one or two checkers from the set. The child who takes away the last checker is the winner. Have the children repeat the activity using a different number of checkers.

High/Low

Your youngsters will enjoy playing this card game as they review the concept greater than/less than. Remove the face cards from a deck of playing cards. Divide the remaining cards equally between a pair of children. Tell each child to place his cards in a stack facedown. Then have both children turn over the top card. The child with the higher number wins both cards. At the end of the game, the player with the most cards is the winner. To extend the activity, tell the children to play the game using the lower number. To vary the activity, use number cards in place of playing cards.

Calculator Fun

This simple game will teach your children how to use a calculator while they review addition facts. Divide children into pairs. Give each child a calculator. Tell each child to take a turn pressing a number between one and five on her calculator. Have her press the plus key after each number is entered to add the numbers together. The first child to reach ten is the winner. If a player's total goes over ten, she starts over. Instruct your children to repeat the activity using the target numbers 12, 15, 18, and 20.

Counting Bugs

Many summer activities involve families taking long trips in the car. Playing the game Bug will entertain the youngsters, as well as sharpen their math skills as they travel. To play the game, each player looks for a Volkswagen Bug. If one is spotted, the player receives one point. If he sees a Volkswagen bus (older-model van), he earns two points. The first player to earn a total of ten points is the winner.

Sorting Socks

Most children will share in household chores while they are at home during the summer months. Set up a center in the classroom where your children can practice a very important household chore: sorting socks. To obtain a large variety of socks for the activity, ask parents and fellow teachers to donate clean, unwanted socks. Place the socks in a laundry basket. Then have the children in a small group sort the socks, match the pairs, and fold them.

Inventory

Let your children assist you in taking the end-of-the-year supply inventory. Use a large sheet of poster board to make an inventory list. Then have pairs of children sort and count small objects such as chalk, erasers, pencils, scissors, bottles of glue, crayons, markers, and books. Instruct the youngsters to count each set of items twice to ensure accuracy. Then record each number on the inventory poster. Your children will take pride in helping their teacher with a grown-up task, and your inventory will be complete in a short amount of time.

Make Ten

Remove the face cards from a deck of playing cards. Give each child in a small group four cards, and place the remainder in a stack facedown in the center of the playing area. Tell the first player to make ten with any combination of any number of cards in his hand. Instruct him to lay down each set making ten and draw enough cards from the stack to give him four again. If there is no possible way for a player to form a set of ten, then he may draw a card (giving him five cards) and see if that allows him to make a set of ten. Have the other children repeat the procedure in turn. At the end of the game, the player with the most combinations of ten is the winner.

How Many Pom-Poms?

Divide a small group of children into pairs. Give each child five pom-poms. Tell one child in each pair to place some of her pom-poms in her hand and make a fist around them. Have her hold out her fist to the other child and ask, "How many?" Tell the other child to guess the number of pom-poms in her hand. If she guesses more than are in the hand, she must give the first child enough pom-poms to make up the difference. If she guesses correctly, she wins all of the pom-poms in the first child's fist. The game is over when one child has all of the pom-poms.

LANGUAGE ARTS

Calendar Activities

Young children enjoy having homework even during summer vacation. Make one copy of the calendar reproducible on page 152 for each of the summer months. Program each day with a different activity such as the ones listed below. Then make a copy of the calendars for each child in the classroom.

Say the alphabet.
Name the days of the week.
Name the months of the year.
Recite a poem.
Draw a picture.

Sing a song.
Read a book.
Tell a story.
Write three
    words on paper.

Road-Trip Fun

Give each child 26 blank cards. Ask her to write a different alphabet letter on each one. Have her place the cards in a stack in alphabetical order. Secure the stack with a rubber band. Encourage her to take the cards with her when she goes on a long trip in the car. Tell her to first look for an *A* on billboards, buildings, and road signs. When one is spotted, instruct her to place the *A* card on the bottom of the stack. Have her repeat the activity with the remaining letter cards.

Thank You

Parent volunteers, administrators, resource teachers, and custodial and cafeteria staff members will be delighted when your children remember them with thank-you notes. Prepare a brief message for each child to copy on a card, or let him write or dictate his own message. Afterwards have him use crayons, markers, or colored pencils to decorate the card.

Word Bank

Have each child make a word bank from a large butter tub or shoebox. Let her decorate the container with paper scraps and stickers. Then cut a slit in the lid. Have her write basic sight words on individual cards and place them inside the word bank. Encourage her to review the words during the summer months. To vary the activity, let younger children make a letter bank.

Summer Reading List

Make a list of books you have read to your class. Draw a star beside each of the class favorites. Send a copy of the list home with each child. Ask parents to choose books from the list to read to their children over the summer. To extend the activity, make a sticker book for each child. Bind several blank pages inside a construction-paper cover. Tell the child to place a sticker in the book each time he reads a book.

Cross Out

Your youngsters will review letter recognition and listening skills as they play the game of Cross Out. Ask each child to write his first and last name on a sheet of paper. Then shuffle a deck of letter cards. Call out the letters one at a time in random order. If a letter appears in the child's name, he crosses it out. If the letter appears more than once in his name, he crosses out each one. The first child to cross out all the letters in both names is the winner. To vary the activity, use sight words instead of names.

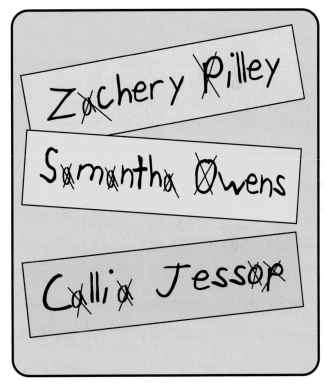

Poetry

Print or type poems you have taught your children on individual sheets of paper. Give one to each child in the classroom. Ask her to use a fine-line marker to illustrate the poem. Gather the poems and make a copy for each child in the classroom. Bind each child's pages together inside a construction-paper cover.

SCIENCE

Bubbles

Every child loves blowing bubbles! Make the following recipe for soap bubbles and pour a portion of the liquid in a small container for each child. Let her make a bubble blower from a pipe cleaner. Then take the class outside for a bubble-blowing extravaganza.

Soap Bubbles

In a container, mix one-part liquid dish detergent with one-part water and stir. Use a bubble blower to blow bubbles. If the soap film breaks easily, add more detergent to the solution until bubbles are produced.

Gross-Motor Games

A variety of gross-motor games that have been played at school can be enjoyed throughout the summer with family and friends. Review each of the following games with your children before school is out for the year:

Hopscotch: Draw a hopscotch diagram similar to the one pictured. Then give each player in a small group a pebble. Tell one player to toss her pebble into box one and hop over it into boxes two and three, placing a foot onto each one. Then have her hop on one foot into box four. Instruct her to continue in the same manner until she reaches box ten. Tell her to jump around in box ten so she is facing the opposite direction. Ask her to hop back through the boxes in the same way

until she reaches boxes two and three. Have her bend over, pick up the pebble, hop into box one, and hop out. Let her then toss her pebble into box two and repeat the activity in the same manner. If a player's pebble does not land in the correct box, if both her feet land in one box, or if a hand or foot touches a line, her turn is over and another player should take a turn. The first player to complete the pattern for all ten boxes wins.

Musical Games: Review the musical games your children have enjoyed such as "The Farmer In The Dell," "London Bridge," and "The Hokey Pokey" before the summer break begins.

Pat-A-Cake Games: Teach your youngsters pat-a-cake games such as "Miss Mary Mack." These gross-motor games can be played at home or while traveling in the car.

Jump-Rope Games: Lay a jump rope on the ground. Tell your children to pretend the rope is a snake. Have them take turns walking on the snake's back. Next lay two jump ropes side by side. Tell each child in a small group to jump over the two ropes. Then gradually increase the distance between the ropes to see how far each child can jump.

SOCIAL STUDIES

My Aunt Came Back

Let your children listen to the song "My Aunt Came Back" from *Barney's Favorites, Vol. 2* CD. Afterwards have them name the items the aunt brought back from her various vacations. Next make a list of several places your children may visit over the summer, such as Disneyland, the beach, the mountains, and a dude ranch. Ask your youngsters to name souvenirs they could bring back from each location and add the items to the list.

Disneyland
beach
mountains
dude ranch
Grand Canyon
Washington, DC

The Public Library

Take your class on a field trip to the public library. Schedule a time for a librarian to share a story with your children and give them a tour of the facility. If possible, arrange for each child who does not have a library card to get one before leaving. Send the library card home with the child along with a note explaining how it is to be used. Encourage all parents to take their children to the library regularly during the summer months.

Time Capsule

If your children made time capsules at the beginning of the school year, take them out of storage. Let each child open his capsule. Then have him compare the contents with examples of his recent work. For example, if a drawing was enclosed, tell him to compare it with a picture he drew recently.

Where Does The Teacher Live?

Most young children think their teachers live at school—even during summer vacation! Read aloud either the book *My Teacher Sleeps In School* by Leatie Weiss or *Where Does The Teacher Live?* by Paula Kurzband Feder. Then show your children a picture of your house or describe where you live. Afterwards give each child a self-addressed, stamped envelope containing a sheet of folded paper. Ask her to write you a letter or draw you a picture while she is at home from school. Tell her how much you will look forward to receiving the letter or picture while you are enjoying vacation at home—not at school.

Dear Mrs. Green,

149

ART

Play Dough

Children enjoy playing with play dough at school and at home. Show a small group of children how they can make play dough with the help of an adult. Ask the children to mix the following ingredients and cook the mixture according to the directions. When the play dough has cooled, give some to each child in the group. Let her mold it into any shape she likes. Send a copy of the recipe home with each child.

Play Dough

2 cups flour
1 cup salt
2 cups water colored with food coloring
2 tablespoons cooking oil
4 teaspoons cream of tartar

Mix the first two ingredients together in a pan. Add the remaining ingredients. Cook on low to medium heat. Scrape the play dough from the sides of the pan as it cooks. When the play dough begins to stiffen, remove it from the pan and place it on a plate to cool. Knead. Store in an airtight container.

Cereal Box Journal

Collect an empty cereal box for each child in the classroom. Cut away the top and narrow sides of each box. Cover it with wrapping paper or Con-Tact paper to create a book cover. Punch two aligned holes in the front and back covers. Then make the pages for the journal by cutting several sheets of newsprint the same size as the book cover. Punch holes in the paper to match the ones in the covers. Thread each end of a piece of heavy yarn or a shoelace through a hole in the back cover, the pages, and the front cover. Tie the ends of the yarn in the front to secure the pages inside the cover. Tell your children to write and/or draw in their journals each week during the summer.

Tie-Dye

Go out in style! Help your children make matching tie-dyed T-shirts to wear on field day or the last day of school. Ask each child to bring in a white T-shirt from home. Tie-dye each shirt by gathering a section of fabric in one hand and wrapping a rubber band around it tightly. Repeat the process as many times as desired. Soak the shirt in water until it is completely wet. Then use a commercial dye to color the shirt according to the package directions. Afterwards rinse the shirt under running water until the water runs clear. Remove the rubber bands and let the T-shirt dry.

You Are My Sunshine

This bulletin board is attractive and can be taken down easily for quick end-of-the-year cleanup. Cover a bulletin board with a sheet of white paper. Print the words "You Are My Sunshine," at the top of the board. Then paint a large sunshine face in the center of the paper. Next give each child a triangular sunshine-ray shape. Tell her to decorate the ray with miscellaneous art supplies, such as aluminum foil, glitter, or sequins. Then have each child sign her name on her ray. Attach the completed rays around the sunshine face. When the school year is over, tear off the paper and throw it away.

SNACK

Celebration Sundae

Let each child celebrate the completion of the school year by making an ice-cream sundae. Place a scoop of ice cream in a bowl for each child. Then let her choose from a variety of toppings such as chocolate chips, M&M's, and candy sprinkles to spoon on the ice cream.

CULMINATING ACTIVITY

Autograph Party

Make a 3" x 5" book with blank pages for each child (the total number of pages in each child's book should equal the number of children in the classroom). Then set aside time on the last day of school for each child to collect the signatures of her classmates. The book will be a keepsake she will read over and over again during the summer months.

School's Out
Open Calendar

Sunday	Monday	Tuesday	Wednesday	Thursday	Friday	Saturday

Note to the teacher: Use with "Calendar Activities" on page 146.

This Land Is Your Land

North, south, east, west—this land is the best. These patriotic ideas and activities about the United States of America are designed to make your children aware of our country's great heritage.

MATH

Counting To Fifty

Each of the fifty states is represented by a star on the United States flag. Lead your class in counting the fifty states on a map and the fifty stars on the flag. Next use manipulatives to help your youngsters count to fifty by ones, fives, and tens. For homework, have each child bring to school a collection of fifty items such as cards, dominos, or pebbles. Have each child share his collection with the class. Then ask one or two volunteers to lead the class in counting the items in his collection.

Lines Of Lincolns

Make three or four gameboards by drawing fifty circles organized in five columns of ten (see below). Supervise a small group of children as they play. First, give each child one of the gameboards. Then place a die and a bowl of 200 pennies in the center. Ask the children to take turns rolling the die and covering the circles with the corresponding number of pennies. The first player to cover all fifty circles is the winner.

Circle The Stars

Give each child in a small group a copy of the reproducible found on page 161. Have the children take turns rolling a die and circling the number of stars rolled. Play continues until one player circles all fifty stars.

Nifty Fifty

On Monday, give each child in the class a copy of the reproducible on page 161. Then have her cross out as many stars as she can in one minute. Ask her to write her name and the number of stars she crossed out on the back of the paper and place it in her cubby. Repeat the activity on Wednesday and Friday. Finally have her compare the number of stars she crossed out on each of the three sheets of paper.

Red, White, And Blue

The colors of our flag each represents a different quality. Red symbolizes *courage,* white stands for *purity* and *innocence,* and blue signifies *vigilance, perseverance,* and *justice.* Cut several sheets of red, white, and blue construction paper into one-inch squares and place them in a learning center. Have the children in the center use the paper squares to make five original patterns. Check each pattern for accuracy.

Climbing The Statue

There are 168 steps from the base of the Statue of Liberty to her crown. Have your children line up in a straight line behind you and count out 168 steps. Time your walk to see how long it would take to reach the top of the Statue of Liberty.

How Big Is She?

The Statue of Liberty stands 151 feet, 1 inch tall. Her index finger is eight feet long. Draw an index finger on an eight-foot-long sheet of paper. Cut out the finger and attach it to a wall in the classroom. Then let each child compare her height with that of the finger.

Thirteen Stripes

The thirteen red and white stripes on the flag symbolize the thirteen original colonies. Have the children in a small group place various felt shapes on a flannelboard to represent the number thirteen. Older children may write several math equations that equal the number thirteen on a chalkboard.

LANGUAGE ARTS

America The Beautiful

Play the song "America The Beautiful" for your children. Then discuss the words to the song. Next have each child create a painting using some of the key phrases. Begin by describing "amber waves of grain" and showing children pictures that might illustrate the phrase. Then have each child paint "amber waves of grain" on a section of white construction paper. Repeat the process for the phrases "purple mountains majesty," "fruited plains," and "spacious skies." Display the completed artwork in the classroom and play the song again as everyone views his classmates' paintings.

Places In America

Obtain several old travel catalogs from a travel agency. Let each child in a learning center look through the catalogs and choose one place in the United States she would like to visit. Then have her draw a picture of that location. When all the pictures have been completed, let each child show her picture to the other children. Ask her to name the place she would like to visit and tell why.

Independence Day

Print the poem "A Rocket In My Pocket," from *The Random House Book Of Poetry For Children* compiled by Jack Prelutsky, on a sheet of chart paper. Read the poem to your children. Then talk about the words in the poem that rhyme, such as *pocket* and *rocket, play* and *day,* and *goes* and *toes.* List the rhyming word pairs on another sheet of chart paper. Next write the words *Independence Day* on a third sheet of chart paper. Have your children think of several smaller words that could be written using the letters in *Independence Day,* and print them on the chart paper.

For a follow-up activity, print each word of the poem on a separate card. Place the poem chart, word cards, and a pocket chart in a learning center. Tell the children in the center to re-create the poem by placing the word cards in the correct order in the pocket chart, using the poem chart as a reference.

155

Field Trip

Plan a field trip to a national landmark in your community. Prior to this trip, discuss the person or event for which the landmark was erected. Afterwards have each child draw a picture of the part of the landmark he liked the most. Then have him write a sentence about his drawing at the bottom of the picture. Bind the pages together to create a class book titled "Our Trip To _____."

What Can We Do?

In his inaugural address, President John F. Kennedy said, "And so, my fellow Americans, ask not what your country can do for you—ask what you can do for your country." Share this quote with your children. Then discuss things they can do to make our country a better place to live. Make a list of all the suggestions. Let each child choose one idea and illustrate it. Then have him write a sentence about his drawing at the bottom of the picture. Bind the pages together to create a class book titled "What We Can Do For Our Country."

A Crack In The Bell

Use the pattern on page 162 to make several bell shapes. Cut out the bells. Cut out pictures from old phonics workbooks. Glue one picture to the left side of each bell. Print the ending sound of the word on the right side of the bell. Cut apart each bell between the picture and the letter. Place the bell halves in a box. Let the children in a small group work together to match the ending sounds with the pictures. To vary the activity, program the bells with initial consonant sounds, upper- and lowercase letters, or compound words.

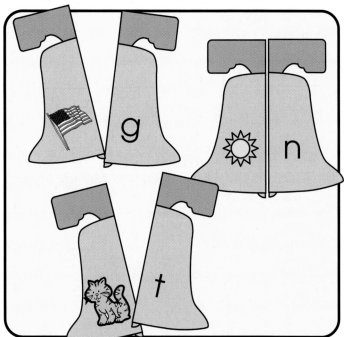

American Paintings

Some say that Norman Rockwell, in his paintings, captured the American spirit better than any other artist in our history. Share a few of his paintings with the children in a small group. Have the children describe the event pictured in each painting. Then ask them to discuss what the people are thinking or doing. Conclude the activity by telling the children the title of each painting. One note: there are several books of Rockwell's paintings available. A good one to use with this activity is *The Faith Of America* with text by Fred Bauer.

SOCIAL STUDIES

Flag Etiquette

Showing respect for the flag is one important way children can demonstrate patriotism. Share the following guidelines for proper flag etiquette with your children. Then ask a pair of Girl Scouts or Boy Scouts to demonstrate how a flag should be raised, lowered, and folded.

1. Stand at attention, look at the flag, and place your right hand over your heart when saying the Pledge of Allegiance.
2. When a flag is raised or lowered or when it passes you in a parade, stand at attention and place your right hand over your heart.
3. Never let the flag touch the ground.
4. Flags that are not in use should be cleaned, properly folded, and stored in a cool, dry place.
5. Flags that are worn beyond repair should be destroyed by burning.

State Symbols

Each state has its own flower, bird, and tree. Show your children a picture of each symbol representative of your state. Then ask them to brainstorm a bird, flower, or tree to represent the class. Let your youngsters vote for their favorite.

Who Or What Am I?

Draw or attach pictures of various American symbols, sights, and people on individual index cards. Pictures may include the flag, the Statue of Liberty, a bald eagle, the Liberty Bell, and a picture of Uncle Sam. In a small-group setting, pin an index card on each child's back without letting him see the picture. Tell him to find out the name of the picture by asking his classmates yes/no questions. Repeat this with each student until everyone knows the name of the picture attached to his back.

Citizenship

Invite a veteran or naturalized citizen to visit your classroom. Ask him to discuss his thoughts and feelings about the United States.

Elections

Invite a Student Council representative in your school to speak to your class. Have him begin by discussing his nomination and campaign strategies. Then ask him to detail the voting process used by his classmates. Finally have him describe the duties and responsibilities of his office. One note: if your elementary school does not have a Student Council, invite a middle school or high school officer to visit your classroom.

SCIENCE

Liberty Bell

The Liberty Bell was made in England and brought to the United States in 1752. Its primary purpose was to announce special events. In 1776 it rang during the signing of the Declaration of Independence. It cracked about 60 years later when it was used to announce the death of Chief Justice John Marshall.

Show your children a picture of the Liberty Bell and briefly describe its history. Then for homework, ask each child to bring in a bell from home. The following day, let everyone ring his bell for the class. Discuss the different sounds and pitches made by the various bells. Then select three bells. Ask your children to arrange them by their pitch from lowest to highest. Label the bells "one" through "three." Place the numbered bells behind a screen and ring them at random. Ask the children to identify each bell by its sound or pitch. Repeat the experiment with different combinations of bells.

The Liberty Bell

Stars

The dark blue field on our nation's flag accentuates the fifty white stars, just as the night sky intensifies the brilliance of the celestial bodies that fill the heavens. Why can we see the stars at night, but not during the day? Demonstrate the answer to this question with the following experiment. Use a hole puncher to make several holes in a card. Place the card inside an envelope. Hold a flashlight close to the front of the envelope and shine the light through it. You cannot see the holes. Now shine the light through the back of the envelope. The holes will be visible because the surrounding area is darker than the light shining through the envelope. Likewise stars can be seen at night because the sky is dark. They cannot be seen during the day because their light blends with that of the sun's.

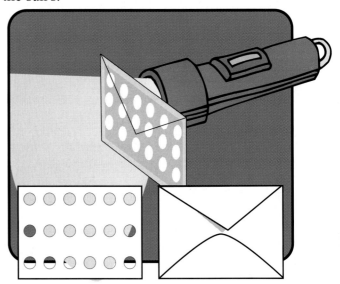

Bald Eagle

Use factual books, such as *A New True Book: Bald Eagles* by Emilie U. Lepthien or *Where The Bald Eagles Gather* by Dorothy Hinshaw Patent, for information concerning the bald eagle. List some important facts about the eagle on a sheet of chart paper and share them with your children. Next discuss the steps taken to prevent this important bird from becoming extinct and list these steps on another sheet of paper. Name other birds and animals that are in danger of becoming extinct. Finally discuss with your children ways they can help these animals.

ART

The Statue Of Liberty

France gave the United States the Statue of Liberty on July 4, 1884. The statue was a symbol of friendship.

Have your class create its own friendship sculpture for your school. Ask your children to bring in cardboard boxes of all shapes and sizes. Then glue and/or tape the boxes together to create an abstract sculpture. Next paint the entire surface with a latex primer or white latex paint to cover the printing on the boxes. Then let the children paint the sculpture with bright-colored paint. Mount the box sculpture on a solid base or hang it from a heavy cord, and display it in the school's lobby.

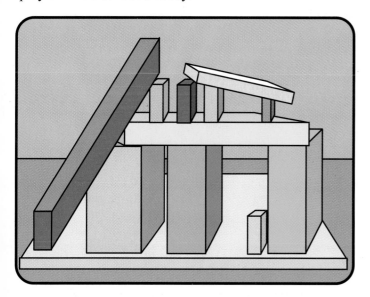

Hand Flag

Make a large hand flag for a hall bulletin board with the help of children from other classes. First cover the bulletin board with white paper. Then draw guidelines on the background paper for the thirteen stripes. Cut out a blue rectangle and attach it to the upper left corner to create the flag's field. Sponge-paint fifty white stars on the blue field. Then ask each child to trace both hands on white and red paper and cut them out. Attach the paper hands to the background paper to create the stripes for the hand flag. Begin by gluing or stapling a row of red hands between the first two guidelines, overlapping the hands to make a solid color. Then repeat the process with a row of white paper hands. Continue the pattern to complete the flag.

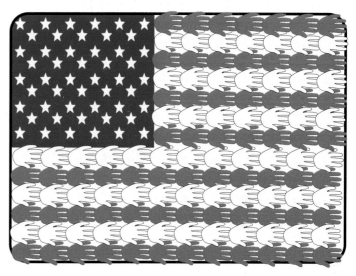

Red, White, And Blue Fireworks

Cover a table in a learning center with newspaper. Give each child in the center a sheet of white construction paper. Let her sprinkle a small amount of red and blue tempera paint in the center of the paper. Next have her place another sheet of white construction paper over the paint. Then—while pressing firmly in the center of the paper with one hand—ask her to rotate the top sheet with one complete turn. Both sheets of paper will have colorful designs representative of fireworks bursting in midair.

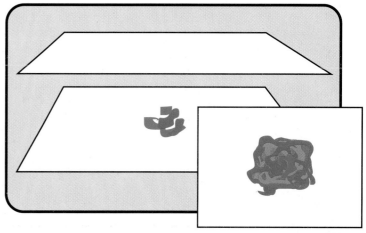

SNACK

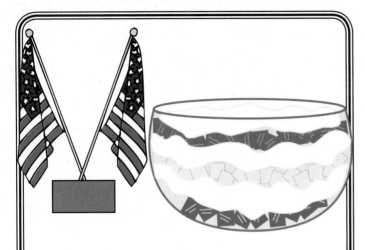

All-American Dessert

1 8-oz. package Berry Blue Jell-O gelatin
1 8-oz. package Strawberry Jell-O gelatin
4 cups boiling water
2 cups cold water
4 cups pound cake cubes
1 8-oz. tub whipped topping, thawed

Dissolve each flavor of gelatin completely in two cups of boiling water in separate bowls. Stir one cup of cold water into each. Pour into separate 13" x 9" pans. Refrigerate three hours or until firm. Cut into 1/2-inch cubes. In a large bowl, layer blue gelatin cubes, one-third of the whipped topping, cake cubes, one-third of the whipped topping, red gelatin cubes, and the remaining whipped topping.

CULMINATING ACTIVITY

Fourth-Of-July Picnic

On the last day of the unit, pretend it is the Fourth of July and time to celebrate our country's birthday. Ask everyone to wear red, white, and blue clothing. Then begin the day by leading the children in the Pledge of Allegiance and a few patriotic songs. Next divide the class into teams and have them participate in relay games such as a sack race and a three-legged race. Complete the celebration with a picnic lunch.

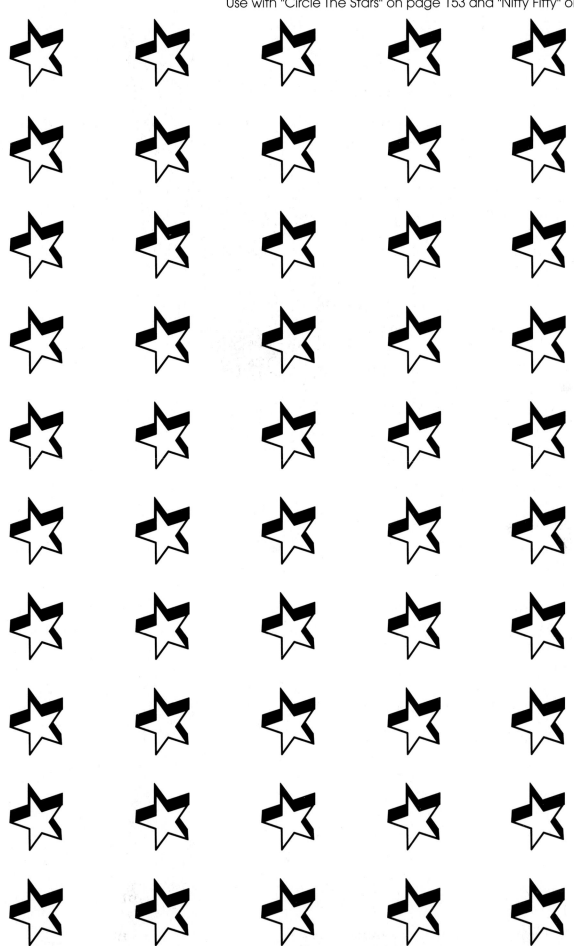

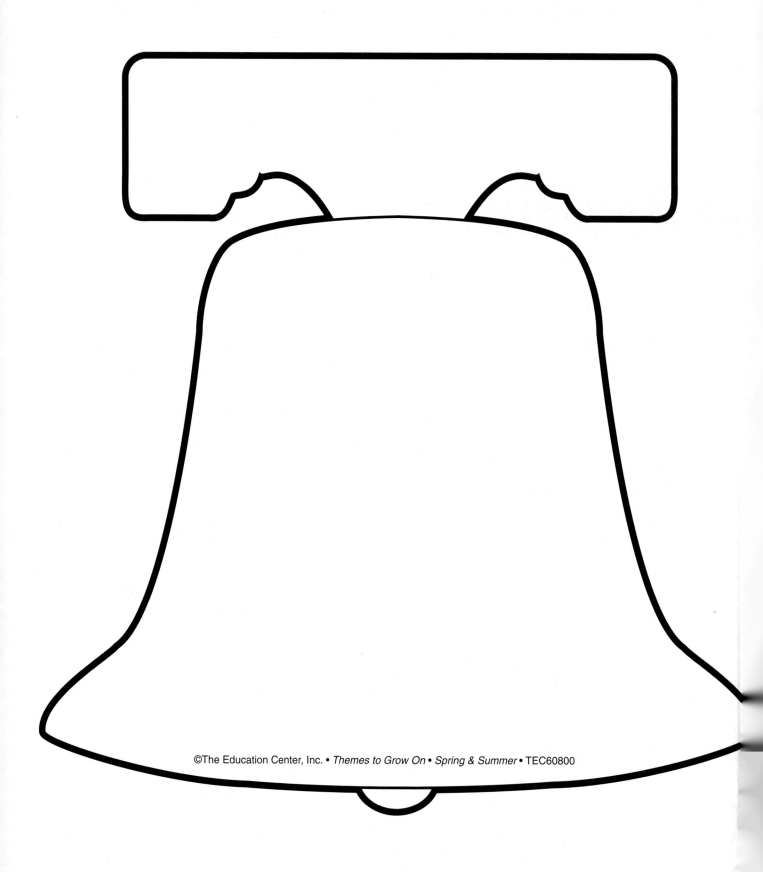

Zoo Animals

Take a walk on the wild side! Join this classroom expedition to the zoo. Your children will discover amazing facts about zoo animals while practicing basic skills.

MATH

Sorting Zoo Animals

Place various plastic animals of all types in a basket. Include dinosaurs, farm animals, pets, and zoo animals. Instruct a small group of children to sort the animals into two groups: zoo animals and animals that don't live in a zoo. Then have them count the number of animals in both groups and tell which has more.

ZOO ANIMALS	OTHER ANIMALS
zebra elephant gorilla lion kangaroo	dog cow pig

Zoo Roll

Your children will review basic math facts as they enjoy this game of chance. Paint several cardboard egg cartons and decorate them with zoo animal stickers. Write a different numeral in the bottom of each egg compartment. Give each child a pom-pom. Have him place it in the carton, close the lid, and shake the carton. Open the carton and observe the numeral on which the pom-pom landed. Tell him to write a problem that equals the number. Instruct him to repeat the activity several times.

Spots And Stripes

Many wild animals have special markings such as spots and stripes to help them hide in their natural environments. Place several paper circles and strips in a learning center. Have the children in the center make several different patterns with the two shapes.

Long Legs

The giraffe is the tallest of all the animals. It gets its height from its legs, which are six feet long. Draw a six-foot giraffe leg. Attach it to a wall in the classroom. Have each child stand beside the leg. Mark his height with a piece of tape. Write the child's name on the tape. Then compare his height with that of the giraffe's leg and his classmates.

PLEASE DO NOT FEED THE ANIMALS

1, 2, 3

Read aloud *1, 2, 3 To The Zoo: A Counting Book* by Eric Carle. Discuss the sequence of the numbers in the book. Next give each of ten student volunteers a number card between one and ten. Have the children stand in random order. Then instruct the group to arrange themselves in the correct numerical order. Finally place three number cards such as *3, 4,* and *6* in a pocket chart. Ask your children to tell which numbers are missing. Repeat the activity using different sets of numbers.

Animal Crackers

How many lions are there in a box of animal crackers? How many zebras? To determine the answers to these and other questions, let your children sort, count, and graph a large box of animal crackers. Make a class graph by attaching an example of each animal cracker on the left-hand side of a grid. Then divide the remaining crackers into individual cups. Give each child a cup. Ask her to sort the animal crackers by kind. Tell her to record the total number of each animal on a sheet of paper. Collect the papers and record the information on the class graph by coloring in a square beside each animal cracker. Finally total the number of animal crackers graphed.

Number Cages

Give each child in a small group a sheet of paper, a pencil, and a crayon. Instruct her to draw three horizontal lines at the top of the paper. Then have her draw three vertical lines over the horizontal ones. Next tell her to use the crayon to color in the squares formed by the intersecting lines. Ask her to count the squares and write the number below each row of squares. Have her repeat the activity by drawing additional vertical lines. To extend the activity, let the children explore new number cages using a set of two, four, or five horizontal lines.

Animal Count

To prepare for this activity, place a container of plastic zoo animals, several containers labeled with zoo animal names, pencils, and sentence strips with the following sentence printed on each strip: "I counted _____ [number] _____ [animals]." Have the children sort the zoo animals into the labeled containers. Then tell them to count the number of animals in each container. Ask each child to record the number and name of each animal group on a sentence strip. For example, "I counted six monkeys." Finally have him read his sentences to another child in the center.

LANGUAGE ARTS

I Like...

Read the poem "Giraffes" by Mary Ann Hoberman from *Animals Animals* by Eric Carle. Discuss the many reasons the author gives for liking giraffes. Then ask each child to name a zoo animal and tell one reason for liking it. For example, "I like monkeys because they swing by their tails." Write each sentence on a sheet of chart paper as it is dictated. Then copy the sentences on individual sheets of paper. Let each child illustrate his sentence. Then bind the papers together to create a class book titled "We Like Zoo Animals."

I like giraffes because they have long necks.

I like monkeys because they swing by their tails.

Zoo Animals' Names

Your children will practice letter-recognition skills while spelling zoo animal names. Give each pair of children in a small group a set of lowercase letter cards. Tell each pair to spread out the cards on the floor or tabletop so they can see each card. Then spell a zoo animal's name using uppercase letters in a pocket chart. Have the children work together to spell the same name using the lowercase letters. Continue in the same manner using other zoo animal names such as *lion, seal, zebra, monkey, tiger, leopard, bear, camel, python, walrus,* and *flamingo.*

Caged Words

Use three plastic strawberry baskets to represent cages. Put a set of consonant letter cards in the first basket, a set of vowel letter cards in the second basket, and another set of consonant cards in the third basket. Instruct a small group of children to use the letter cards to make three-letter words such as *dog, cat, sun,* and *top.* One note: color code each letter card for easy sorting and include duplicate cards for letters that are used frequently such as *t, n,* and the vowels.

Describing The Zoo

Read aloud *A Children's Zoo* by Tana Hoban. Discuss the three words used to describe each zoo animal pictured in the book. Then let your youngsters create a similar class book using the same format. Cut out pictures of zoo animals from magazines such as *Ranger Rick* or *National Geographic.* Glue the pictures on individual sheets of paper. Let each child choose one picture and think of three words to describe it. Print the words on the paper. Then bind the papers together to create a class book titled "Children's Zoo."

PLEASE DO NOT FEED
THE ANIMALS

Python Rhyming Words

Ask your children to help you make lists of rhyming words on chart paper. Then give each child a copy of the python reproducible on page 171. Have him color the python's head and tail and cut out both shapes. Then give him a piece of paper that has been fan-folded (as shown). Instruct him to choose rhyming words from the list and copy each word in a section of the folded paper. Tell him to glue the python's head to the top of the paper and the tail to the bottom.

Rebus Book

Give each child a copy of the reproducible on page 172. Have her cut apart the rebus sentences on the solid black lines. Next tell her to glue each sentence in the correct order at the bottom of a sheet of paper. Ask her to illustrate each sentence. Then bind the pages inside a bright-colored, construction-paper cover to create an individual book titled "The Zoo Book."

Zoo Box

Paint a large cardboard box to resemble a cage. Then place several objects in the box. (The name of each object should begin with a different initial consonant sound.) Take the objects out of the box one at a time and place them on the floor. As you do this, ask your children to name each object and its beginning sound. When all the objects have been removed from the box, help your children place them in alphabetical order.

Animal ABC

Your youngsters will want to play this card game again and again. To prepare for the game, write the letters of the alphabet on a sheet of chart paper (omit the letter x). Then ask your children to think of the name of a zoo animal that begins with each letter. Write the names beside the appropriate letters. Then copy each name on an individual word card. Shuffle the cards and place them facedown in the center of a table. Ask a small group of children to sit around the table. Instruct each child to take one card from the top of the stack and show it to the others. The child with the letter that comes first in the alphabet may take the others' cards. Tell the children to repeat the procedure until all the cards have been played. At the end of the game, the child with the most cards is the winner.

SCIENCE

Sloth
lives in trees
mammal
round head
hangs upside down
claws
long arms

Observing The Unusual

Collect several pictures of unusual zoo animals such as the sloth, the platypus, and the lemur. Let your children observe one of the pictures and describe the animal. Make a list of the observations as they are shared. Then cover up the picture and the list. Ask your youngsters to think of the words used to describe the animal in the first list and to make a second list. Afterwards uncover the picture and the first list. Compare the information on the first list with that on the second. Then tell your children the animal's name, and give them some background information on it. Repeat the activity with the remaining pictures.

What Do You Hear?

Read aloud *Polar Bear, Polar Bear, What Do You Hear?* by Bill Martin, Jr. Then stand behind a screen or ask your children to put their heads down on their desks, and make several sounds such as dropping a book, writing on the chalkboard, and crumpling a sheet of paper. Ask your children to identify each sound. Then for homework, ask each child to think of one sound she could make. On the following day, let her make the sound behind the screen, and ask the other children to guess what it is.

Zoo Food

Feeding the zoo animals is a very important job for the zookeeper. Each animal must be given the correct amount of food that contains the right mixture of nourishing ingredients. For more information about feeding zoo animals, read *Understanding Zoo Animals* edited by Rosamund Kidman Cox and Barbara Cork. Next print the following headings on a sheet of chart paper: "Plant Eater—Giraffe," "Meat Eater—Lion," "Insect Eater—Anteater," and "Mixed Feeder—Galago." Under each heading, write examples of foods used to feed the animal. Then prepare a zoo snack for your children with a food from each category (*meat*—hot dogs cut in thin strips or pepperoni, *plants*—parsley or lettuce, *insects*—chocolate chips, *mixed*—Cheerios).

Zoo Babies

To introduce your children to baby zoo animals, read the book *The Baby Zoo* by Bruce McMillan. Then ask your children to help you list the baby animal names such as *calf, cub,* and *kid.* Have your youngsters think of other baby animals which have the same names and add them to the list. Finally make a book of baby animal names by writing each one on a sheet of paper. Then have your children draw or glue pictures of baby animals with that name on each paper.

SOCIAL STUDIES

Field Trip

Plan a field trip to a local zoo. If a zoo is not located near your school, let your children watch a video showing zoo life. Afterward discuss the duties and responsibilities of various zoo workers such as the veterinarian, the dietitian, the groundskeepers, and the concession workers. Ask each child to draw a picture of one worker performing his job at the zoo. Display the pictures on a bulletin board.

Scott

Locate On A Map

Many zoo animals lived in faraway lands before coming to live in the zoo. Attach pictures of common zoo animals—such as an elephant, a giraffe, and a chimpanzee—around a world map. Locate the natural habitat of each animal on the map. Match it to the picture of the animal with a piece of yarn. Display the map in the classroom for the duration of the unit.

Adopt An Animal

Help your children become better acquainted with a desert tortoise, a warthog, or a screech owl. Many zoos have an adopt-an-animal program that will provide your children with learning opportunities throughout the school year. Check local zoos or nature science centers for program information.

"The Lion And The Mouse"

Read aloud "The Lion And The Mouse" from *City Mouse-Country Mouse And Two More Tales From Aesop* illustrated by John Wallner. Discuss how the tiny mouse helped the mighty lion. Then ask your youngsters to think of ways children can help adults. List the ideas on a sheet of chart paper. Tell each child to choose one idea and illustrate it on a sheet of paper. Let her share her picture with the class. Ask other children to guess what is happening in the picture.

ART

Big Cat Origami

Read aloud *Have You Seen My Cat?* by Eric Carle. Then ask your children to name each cat pictured in the book. Have them describe its distinctive coloring. Next let each child create an origami cat using these simple directions. Fold a piece of paper diagonally. Fold the outer corners down, then up. Turn the paper over. Fold the top layer of the bottom corner up to create the mouth. Use markers to make the eyes, nose, whiskers, and special markings.

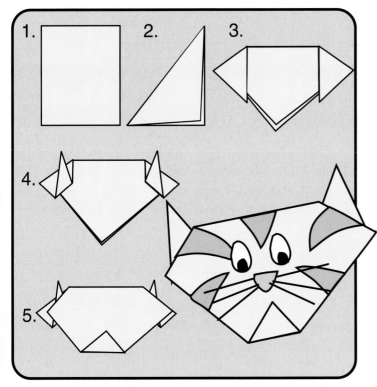

Cookie-Cutter Animals

To prepare for this activity, collect a quantity of zoo animal cookie cutters. Next pour different colors of liquid tempera paint into individual trays. Place the cookie cutters, trays of paint, construction paper, and Q-tips in a learning center. Tell each child to choose a cookie cutter, press it into the paint, and print an animal shape on a sheet of paper. Have him repeat the procedure using other cookie cutters. Let him use Q-tips dipped in paint to add features to the animals.

Zebra Stripes

Create an attractive zebra stripes design by printing black on white. To prepare for the activity, make a printing block for each child in a small group. Wrap jute twine around a wooden block and tie in the back. (Make sure there is space between the strands of twine.) Tell each child to dip her block into a tray of black tempera paint. Then have her press it on a sheet of white construction paper to create the stripes. Instruct her to repeat the procedure several times. When the paint is dry, mount the print on a black sheet of construction paper. To vary the activity, use white tempera paint and black paper.

Animal Masks

Let each child create an animal mask using construction paper, scissors, markers, yarn, and a cereal box. Collect a quantity of cereal boxes. Cut off the back and the bottom side of each box. Next give each child a sheet of construction paper. Have her draw the outline of an animal's face on the paper and cut it out. Tell her to use paper scraps and markers to decorate the face. Then mount it on the front of a cereal box as shown. Cut the front of the box to match the shape of the face. Cut holes for the eyes. Then punch a hole in each side of the box and thread a piece of yarn through each hole. Fit the mask on the child's head and tie the yarn in the back.

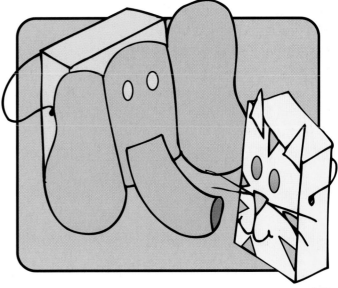

169

SNACK

Python Cookies

Soften a tube of slice-and-bake cookie dough.
Roll the cookie dough into a ball. Add ten drops
of food coloring and mix. (The food coloring
will not mix thoroughly, creating stripes in
the cookies.) Roll out the cookie dough into a
1/4-inch-wide strand. Cut the strand into 6-inch
pieces. Shape each piece into an *s*-shape. Press
in two small candies for the eyes. Bake according
to package directions.

CULMINATING ACTIVITY

Zany Zoo

Let each child participate in the creation of a zany
zoo. Ask her to sculpt a zoo animal from a ball of
clay. Let the clay figure harden. Then have her paint
it an unusual color. Display the zany zoo in the classroom, media center, or school showcase.

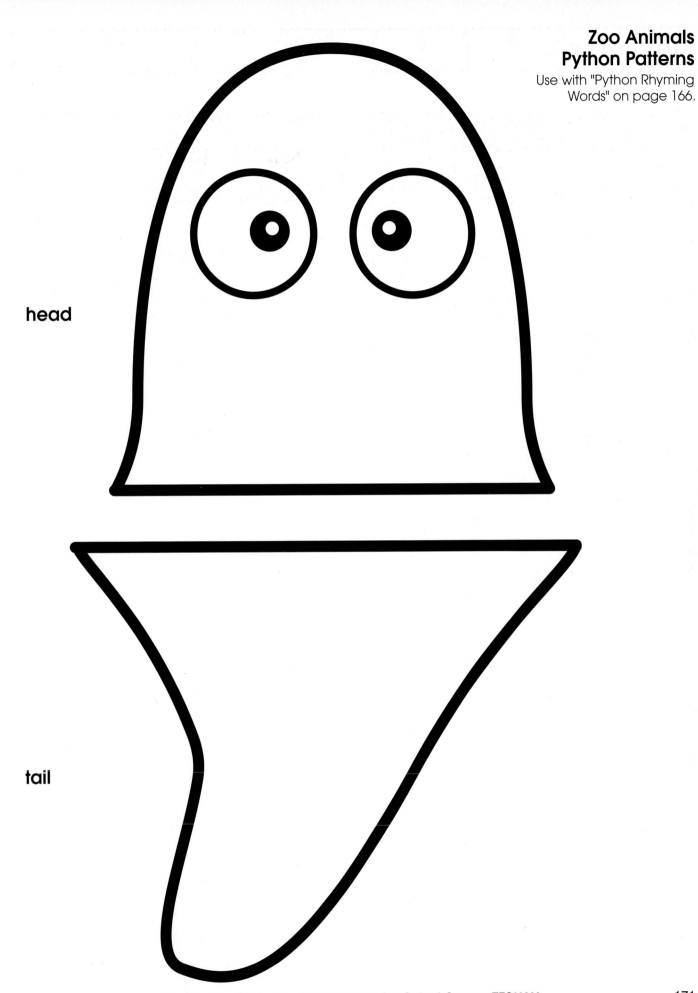

head

tail

The	is	in	the		ZOO .
The	is	in	the		ZOO .
The	is	in	the		ZOO .

Space

All systems are go for a cosmic adventure into space. Ignite the imaginations of your children as they embark on a far-out exploration of space travel and the solar system.

MATH

Craters On The Moon

Explain what a crater is and show an illustration of craters. Cut out several paper circles to represent moons. Use a hole puncher to make a different number of holes or craters in each one. Place one circle at a time on an overhead projector. Ask your children to tell how many craters are on each moon by counting the number of holes in each circle.

Jupiter And Pluto

Jupiter is the largest planet in our solar system and Pluto is the smallest. Place several containers of objects such as pencils, crayons, chalk, and blocks in a learning center. Ask the children in the center to find the largest and the smallest object in each container. To vary the activity, tell the youngsters to put each container of objects in order from the smallest to the largest.

Moon Walk

Let your children pretend to walk on the moon as they identify numerals and colors. On an old bedsheet, draw several circles to represent craters on the moon. Use colored markers to write a different numeral in each circle. Place the sheet and a pair of oversized, furry slippers in a learning center. Have each child wear the slippers as he uses exaggerated steps to follow your oral directions and walk on the sheet. Tell him to step on each crater and name the color and numeral, such as yellow fifteen or blue nine. The moon walk ends when all of the colors and numerals have been named or when one is named incorrectly.

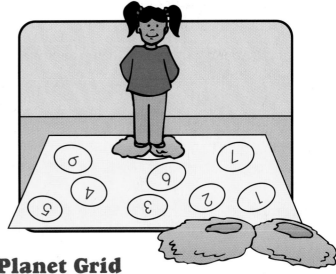

Planet Grid

Make several copies of the grid on page 181. Place the grids, colored pencils, and nine different-sized planet patterns in a center. Tell each child to choose two or three patterns and trace them on the grid. Next have him color the planets by coloring each whole square one color and each partial square another color. Finally ask him to count the whole squares to see which planet covered the most and which planet covered the least area.

173

The Solar System

The planets in our solar system orbit around the Sun in the following order: Mercury, Venus, Earth, Mars, Jupiter, Saturn, Uranus, Neptune, and Pluto. Reinforce ordinal number word sequence with this activity. Cut out a poster-board circle to represent each of the nine planets. Write the name of each of the nine planets on a cutout. Give nine children one planet shape each. Help them arrange themselves in the correct order. Ask the third child to step forward and call out the name of his planet. Continue this procedure until all the planets have been named. Then let another group of children have a turn. To extend the activity, let each child make a foldout book of the solar system. Fan-fold a strip of paper to make ten sections. Write the title "Solar System," and the child's name on the first section. Then have him draw or attach a cutout of a planet to each of the remaining sections and copy each planet's name on the appropriate section.

Countdown March

Have your youngsters count forward and backward as they march around a table to the music of Hap Palmer's "The Number March" from the record *Learning Basic Skills Through Music: Volume I.* Before the march begins, label five children with a number between one and five. Tell the children to stand beside the table. Begin the record. When she hears her number named in the song, have each child march around the table. Have her sit down when she hears her number named a second time. Repeat the activity with another group of children.

Solar Toss

Your children will have a blast reviewing basic math facts while playing a tossing game. To prepare for the game, make cutouts of the Sun, Earth, and Moon. Attach each cutout to an empty wastebasket. Place the wastebaskets in a line at an equal distance apart. Have the children in a small group take turns tossing a beanbag at the wastebaskets. If the beanbag lands in the first wastebasket, one point is scored; if it lands in the second one, two points are scored; and if it lands in the third wastebasket, three points are scored. Have each child keep a running total of her score. At the end of the game, the child with the most points is the winner.

Starlight

Make several copies of the star reproducible on page 182. Write a different numeral in the center of each star. Then write a different math fact equal to the numeral in each star's ray. Laminate the stars for durability. Next cut each one apart on the solid lines to create a puzzle. Place the puzzle pieces in a container. Have a small group of children re-create the stars by placing the rays around the correct centers.

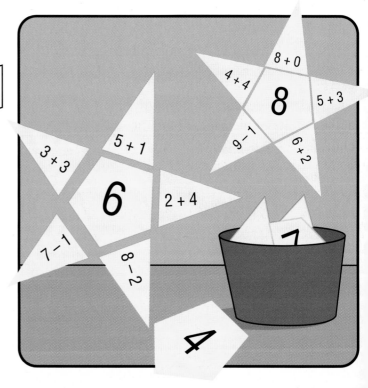

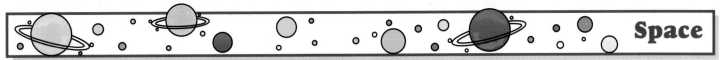
LANGUAGE ARTS

Lost In Space

Use this simple game to review the letters of the alphabet. Choose one letter from a deck of alphabet cards. Show the letter to the class. This letter will be considered the lost letter. Say the letter's name with your children. Then shuffle the letter card in with the remaining alphabet cards. Show one letter card to your youngsters at a time. Ask them to clap twice when they see the lost letter. Repeat the activity using a different letter.

Clouds

Clouds are something that astronauts can see from space as they look at earth or other planets. Read aloud *It Looked Like Spilt Milk* by Charles G. Shaw. Then discuss how clouds can sometimes look like certain objects. Next take your children outside. Ask them to look closely at the clouds in the sky and point out any that resemble objects. When you go back into the classroom, let each child create her own cloud. Give her a sheet of dark blue construction paper that has been folded in half vertically. Tell her to open the paper and spoon white tempera paint along the folded line. Then have her refold the paper and rub it from the fold outward to spread the paint. Tell her to open the paper and look at the interesting cloud that she created. Ask her to describe what her cloud looks like. Then print the sentence, "It looks like_____," at the bottom of the page. Fill in the blank with the child's reply. When the paint dries, bind the papers together to make a class book titled "Clouds."

It looks like popcorn.

Flying Saucers

This UFO activity will help your children listen for beginning, middle, and ending letter sounds. Give each child in a small group a container of cereal and three small paper plates. Tell him to pretend the plates are flying saucers and the cereal pieces are aliens. Next have him label one of the plates "B" for beginning, one plate "M" for middle, and one plate "E" for ending. Then say a word such as *hat*. Ask the child to indicate where he hears the *t* sound by placing an alien in the appropriate flying saucer. Repeat the procedure with other CVC-pattern words. At the conclusion of the activity, let the children eat the cereal.

Twinkle, Twinkle

Print the poem "The Star" by Jane Taylor, from *Read-Aloud Rhymes For The Very Young* selected by Jack Prelutsky, on a sheet of chart paper. Use the chart to teach the poem to your children. Then copy each word on an individual card. Place the chart, the word cards, and a pocket chart in a learning center. Tell the children in the center to re-create the poem by placing the word cards in the pocket chart in the correct order.

Burn Out

Print the following words on individual cards: *cat, fan, star, hen, pet, red, sit, pin, sing, will, mop, sun, cake, tail, read, bee, pie, like,* and *go.* Place the cards in a stack facedown in the center of a table. Assemble a small group of children around the table. Have one child pick up the top card, read the word, and say another word that rhymes with it. If he is successful, tell him to pass the card to the next child. Have the child think of an additional rhyming word. Play continues until one child is unable to name a rhyming word and "burns out." Ask the children to repeat the activity using the next card. To vary the activity, read a word to the group of children. Ask them to name several words that rhyme with it. Then repeat the procedure with the remaining words.

Logbook

Astronauts keep a daily log or journal of their activities while in space. Let each child keep a similar log during the week of the Space unit. To make a logbook, staple five blank pages inside a construction-paper cover. Have each child make a daily entry in his book by writing a sentence and/or drawing a picture on one of the pages. At the end of the week, have him share his logbook with a partner.

Star Bright

Make five copies of the star reproducible on page 182. Print a different vowel in the center of each star. Write a different word with that short vowel sound in each star's ray. Laminate the stars for durability. Then cut apart each star on the solid black lines to create a star puzzle. Place the puzzle pieces in a container. Tell the children in a small group to re-create the five stars by joining the rays to the appropriate star centers.

Draw Me A Star

Read aloud *Draw Me A Star* by Eric Carle. After reading the story, have your children name each thing drawn by the artist in the story. List each item on a sheet of chart paper. Then make a set of cards with the following sentence printed on each one: "Draw me a _____." Fill in the blank with the words from the list (include additional words such as *box, girl,* and *rainbow* if more cards are needed). Place the cards, a *large* sheet of paper, tempera paints, and brushes in a center. Have small groups of children use the materials in the center to create a mural similar to the one in the book. Ask each child to choose a card, read the directions, and paint a corresponding picture on the paper. When everyone has had a turn, attach the mural to a bulletin board. Then staple the cards around the mural to create a border your children can read.

SCIENCE

Gravity

Gravity is like a strong invisible glue that holds us to the earth's surface. There is no gravity in space, so the astronauts need restraints to hold them in place inside the shuttle cabin. To demonstrate the force of gravity, have each child pull himself up to a chinning bar. As he feels his muscles strain to pull the weight of the body upward, explain that gravity is pulling him downward.

Space Snacks

In space what astronauts eat and how they eat are different because of the lack of gravity. Crumbs or liquids that spill do not fall to the ground. They float around in the shuttle cabin. Let each child in a small group test the following snack foods to determine which one would be the best choice for a space snack: a cracker, a cookie, a marshmallow, and a potato chip. Give each child four napkins and each of the four snack foods. Tell her to hold a napkin under her chin and take a bite out of the cracker. Have her catch the crumbs with her napkin and place the napkin on the table. Instruct her to repeat the procedure with the other foods. Afterwards ask her to compare the amount of crumbs from each food to decide which snack is best for space travel.

Sun, Earth, Moon

Place a large beach ball, a marble, and a pea on a table in front of the class. Tell your children the beach ball represents the Sun, the marble represents the Earth, and the pea represents the Moon. Ask them which is larger: the Sun or the Moon? The Earth or the Sun? The Moon or the Earth? Then give each child a lump of molding clay. Tell her to use the clay to make balls representative of the Sun, Earth, and Moon.

Balloon Rocket

Cut a plastic drinking straw in half. Thread a ten-foot piece of string through it. Tie the string to the backs of two chairs. Position the chairs as shown to make the string as tight as possible. Slide the straw to one end of the string. Inflate a balloon and hold it shut with your fingers while you tape it as shown to the straw. Tape a penny to the bottom of the ballon for weight. Then release the balloon. It will be propelled along the string until it deflates. Remove the balloon from childrens' reach when finished.

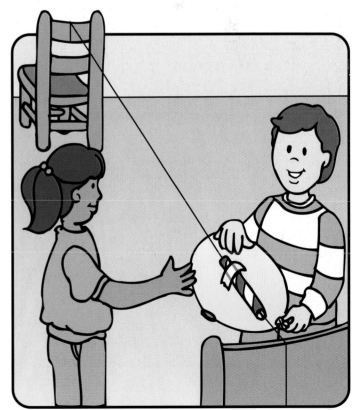

177

SOCIAL STUDIES

Day And Night

Tell your children to stand in a straight line, one behind the other. Mount a cutout of the Sun on the wall facing the children. Mount a cutout of the Moon to the right of the sun. Then read aloud the first statement listed below. Ask each child to take one step to the left if she usually performs the activity during the day. If she usually does it at night, have her take one step to the right. After she has responded to the statement, have her step back in line. Repeat the activity with the remaining statements.

I go to school.	I eat lunch.
I take a bath.	I go to bed.
I eat breakfast.	I do my homework.
I put on my pajamas.	I get dressed.
I play outside.	I eat dinner.

The Right Stuff

Read aloud *I Can Be An Astronaut* by June Behrens. Then ask your children to describe what it takes to be an astronaut. List each idea on a sheet of chart paper. Afterwards tell your youngsters they can earn stars toward becoming junior astronauts. Give each child a round badge. During the week, place a gummed star on the badge for each of the following tasks performed:

Count backwards from ten to one.
Run one lap around the playground.
Name at least three planets.
Do one chin-up.

Shuttle Space

Astronauts must live and work in confined areas while aboard a space shuttle. Tape off an area in the classroom. Tell your youngsters to pretend the area is the interior of a space shuttle. Let a different small group of children work in the area for a certain amount of time each day. At the end of the week, discuss the pros and cons of working in such a small area.

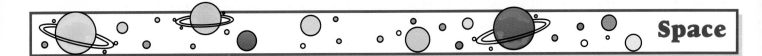

ART

Paper Bag Helmet

Your children will enjoy making helmets similar to those worn by astronauts. Obtain a paper grocery bag for each child in the class. Trace a 6" x 8" oval pattern onto one side, near the bottom of each bag. Cut out the oval shape. Cut a half-circle from each side of the bag, as shown, to fit over the child's shoulders. Then let the child use markers, stickers, and paper scraps to decorate the helmet.

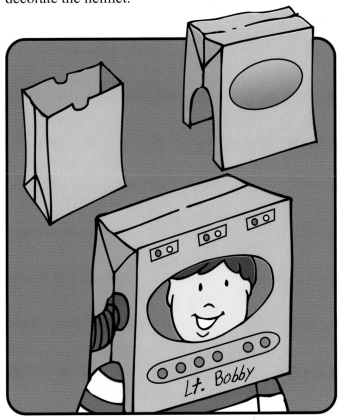

Shape Shuttle

Use a paper cutter to cut several sheets of construction paper into squares, rectangles, and triangles. Place the shapes in a learning center. Tell each child in the center to create a space shuttle using some of the shapes. Then have him glue the shuttle pieces to a sheet of paper. Let each child use markers, stickers, or glitter to decorate his shuttle.

Textured Planets

The Earth's surface is very different from the surfaces of the other eight planets in our solar system. Mercury is bare, rocky, and covered with craters; Venus is a hot desert with a plain, huge mountains, canyons, and volcanoes; Mars is rocky and has several canyons and volcanoes; Jupiter is a large ball of hot liquid surrounded by gas; Saturn, Uranus, and Neptune seem to be large balls of gas and ice; and Pluto looks bare and frozen. Let your youngsters create textured planets using a variety of materials such as cornmeal, rice, oatmeal, coffee grounds, cereal, and eggshells. Give each child a planet shape cut from poster board. Let her glue the supplied materials to the planet cutout to create rocks, craters, and other special features. Let the planets dry; then arrange them on a bulletin board or hang them from the ceiling in the classroom.

UFO

Show your children how to make UFOs that really fly. To prepare for the activity, create a pattern for each child by cutting four half-circles from the perimeter of a paper plate as shown. Have him trace the pattern on five other paper plates. Then cut out the half-circle shapes. Next tell him to stack and match the paper plates. Staple them together. Finally let him use stickers, paper scraps, or markers to decorate the UFO. Throw the UFO like a Frisbee to make it fly.

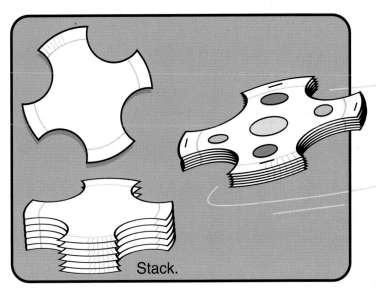

Stack.

SNACK

Meteorites

Soften a tube of slice-and-bake sugar cookie dough. Mix in colorful sprinkles and crushed hard candies. Shape into balls. Bake according to package directions.

CULMINATING ACTIVITY

Egg Drop

Space shuttles are designed to protect their cargo during takeoffs and landings. Show your children an egg. Ask them to pretend it is the cargo aboard a space shuttle. For homework, ask each child to design and build a container that would protect an egg during a fall. Then test each container by placing an egg inside it and dropping it from a certain height.

Space Pattern
Use with "Starlight" on page 174 and "Star Bright" on page 176.

Under The Sea

Dive into a week of adventure exploring the mysteries of the sea! Create a seaside environment in your classroom that will invite children to discover a world of sand, shells, and sea life.

MATH

Schools Of Fish

Seat a small group of students at a table. Give each child twelve Goldfish crackers. Assist children in following the directions listed below to create different schools of fish. Be sure to tell children that they will not use all of the crackers for each direction.

Make five rows of two.
Make three rows of three.
Make six rows of two.
Make two rows of four.
Make eight rows of one.
Make two rows of three.

Make four rows of two.
Make three rows of four.
Make two rows of six.
Make one row of twelve.
Make three rows of two.
Make four rows of three.

Treasure Chest

Decorate a large shoebox with a lid to resemble a treasure chest. Then place an assortment of charms, colored macaroni, and several plastic strings in the box. In a learning center, have children use the things in the box to make necklaces and bracelets with various patterns. (Provide supervision as needed.)

Sailing, Sailing

Place several containers of various sizes (that a toy boat would comfortably fit into), a measuring cup, and a toy boat in a learning center. Tell the children in the center to put the boat in one of the containers. Then predict how many cups of water it will take to make the boat rise to the top of the container. Once the predictions have been made, let the children pour water by the cupful into the container to see how many are needed. Ask the youngsters to repeat the procedure using the other containers.

Sizing Up Shells

Place a bucket filled with a variety of shells in a learning center. Let the children sort the shells by size, placing the small, medium, and large shells on three separate trays. Finally let the children use a set of scales to compare the shells. They may, for example, put a large shell on one side of the scales and see how many small shells they need to put on the other side to balance the scales.

Buried Treasure

Place several shoeboxes filled with sand on a table. Bury several pennies, shells, or pieces of old costume jewelry in the boxes. Assemble a small group of children around the table. Give each of them a shoebox and tell them that the boxes contain buried treasure. You may also say how many pieces of buried treasure each of the boxes contains and have children hunt until all of the pieces are found. Another variation is to give the children a time limit to hunt for the treasure. When the time is up, have them discuss who found the most treasure, the least, and so forth.

Buckets Of Shells

Collect ten sand buckets and number them one to ten. Put the buckets and a box of at least 55 shells in a learning center. Instruct the children to count out the appropriate number of shells and place them in each bucket.

Goldfish Arithmetic

Begin by cutting a piece of tagboard into several strips. Write different addition and subtraction problems on the front and back of each strip ($2 + 3 =$ _____, $4 - 2 =$ _____, etc.). Then laminate the strips for durability. Place the laminated strips and several grease pencils in a learning center along with a bowl of Goldfish crackers. Tell the children to use the crackers to help them solve the math problems. Have them write the answers in the blanks with the grease pencils. Allow the children to eat a few of the crackers as they work.

Goldfish Cracker Predicting

Fill a large container with an assortment of pretzel, cheese, and plain Goldfish crackers. Ask each child to estimate how many crackers are in the container. Have him write his name and estimation on a sheet of paper. Then have each child fill a small paper cup with crackers from the container and sit in a small group. Let him sort and count the various kinds of Goldfish crackers. List the categories on the chalkboard, the overhead, or a large graph. Ask the children in each group to count the total number of crackers in each category, and write the number under the category. Add the numbers in each category together to see how many are in each one. Then add the totals together to determine the number of Goldfish crackers in the container. See whose estimates were the closest.

LANGUAGE ARTS

Sand Writing

Write several letters of the alphabet on individual cards. Have each child in a small group pick a letter and trace over it using glue. Then have each child place her letter card inside a box lid. Let the child sprinkle sand over the letter until it is covered completely. Finally have the child lift the letter card out of the lid and carefully shake off the excess sand so that only the letter is covered. When the glue dries, the child can run her fingers over the sand letter to feel its shape. To vary this activity, use each child's name or simple sight words.

Silent Reading

Set up a reading corner in your classroom complete with beach towels and beach bags filled with books about the sea. Allow small groups of children to visit the corner at various times during the week.

Fishing For Letters

Create a fishing game by duplicating the fish pattern (see page 191) on bright-colored construction paper. You may want to make 26 fish and write a different alphabet letter on the back of each, or make fewer fish and write sight words on their backs. Laminate the fish, cut them out, and attach a paper clip to each of their mouths.

To make the fishing pole, attach a long piece of string to a pole and tie a magnet to the end of the string. Then place the fish on the floor so the alphabet letters or words are facedown, and have a small group of children stand in a circle around them. Tell children to take turns catching fish by holding the fishing pole over a fish so that the magnet touches the paper clip. Once a child catches a fish, he must read what is written on the back. If correct, he keeps the fish. If not, he puts it back. At the end of the activity, have children who have caught alphabet fish place them in alphabetical order. Have those who caught sight-word fish try to make simple sentences using some of the words.

A House For Hermit Crab

Read aloud Eric Carle's *A House For Hermit Crab*. Have the children name the things that Hermit Crab gathered to decorate his shell, listing the names in order on chart paper. Once the list is complete, give each child a picture of Hermit Crab (see page 192). Tell children to color the picture and decorate it any way they wish. Let children share their creations with the class. Then bind the papers together in a class book.

185

Wishes

Read aloud *The Magic Fish* adapted by Freya Little-dale. Have your students discuss the foolish wishes made by the fisherman and his wife. Then ask them to think of wise wishes the pair could have made. Once the discussion is over, give each child a piece of paper that has been folded in half lengthwise. Have him draw a picture of something that would be a foolish wish on one half of the paper and something that would be a wise wish on the other half. Let him share his two wishes with the other children.

The Bottom Of The Sea

Lead your children in singing "There's A Hole In The Bottom Of The Sea" from the CD *Disney's Silly Songs*. Then have your youngsters say each of the things named in the song that are at the bottom of the sea. Next place a picture of each thing in random order in front of the class. Have student volunteers place the pictures in the correct sequence. Finally ask a small group of children to stand in a line. Give each child one of the pictures. Then lead the class in singing the song again. Have each child in the small group hold up her picture when it is mentioned in the song.

Tongue Twisters

Print the tongue twister "If Neither He Sells Sea-shells"—from *A Twister Of Twists, A Tangler Of Tongues* collected by Alvin Schwartz—on a sheet of chart paper. Read the tongue twister aloud to your class. Then have your children read it with you. Next ask your youngsters to name each word in the poem that begins with an *s* or *sh.* As each word is named, circle it with a red marker. Repeat the procedure with other tongue twisters. Then discuss reasons why this type of poem is so difficult to say.

Rhyming Book

Have your children think of words that rhyme with *shell.* Print the words on chart paper as they are dictated by the children. Next give each child three sea-shell cutouts. Ask her to choose three of the rhyming words and draw a picture of each on one of the sheets of paper. Have her label each picture. Then bind the pages inside a shell-shaped cover.

SCIENCE

Seawater Jar

Give each child in a small group an empty baby food jar. Have him place a small shell, some tiny pebbles, and a handful of sand in his jar. Then pour water in the jar until it is approximately three-fourths full. Secure the lid tightly and tell him to shake the jar vigorously. Finally have him place the jar on a table and watch carefully to see what will happen.

Fresh Water And Saltwater

Pour two cups of tap water in a small, deep, clear container. In a similar container, pour two cups of very warm water and add six to seven tablespoons of salt. Stir until the salt dissolves and let the water cool slightly. Place a raw egg in the container of tap water and it will sink. Then place the same egg in the container of saltwater and it will float.

Animal Differences

Talk about the differences between animals that live on land and those that live in water. Then have your children look through old magazines and cut out pictures of both types of animals. Paste the pictures on two separate posters.

Beautiful Shells

Put several shells in small shoeboxes, and place them in a learning center. Give one box to each child at the center. Tell the children to look at their shells very carefully, observing each shell's unique features. Then assist each child in completing a lab sheet (see page 191). Have him share his results with the others in the group.

Pollution

Prepare a demonstration to illustrate the effects of pollution. First fill two mayonnaise jars with clear tap water. Show the jars of water to your students. Then pour several "pollutants" into one jar. Ask the children which of the two jars they would want to live in if they were fish. Let this simple activity be a springboard for discussing how oceans become polluted and what we can do to help make them clean.

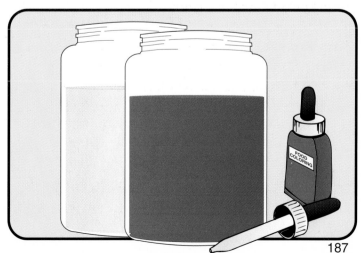

SOCIAL STUDIES

Class Aquarium

Enjoy the beauty of the sea in your own classroom. Set up a classroom aquarium. Provide the tank and filtering device. Then ask student volunteers to donate small items such as seashells, marbles, plastic seaweed, fish, and fish food. Assign a different helper to feed the fish and clean the aquarium each week.

Sea Jobs

The sea provides many jobs, such as those of divers, fishermen, lifeguards, marine biologists, treasure hunters, sailors, truckers, and restaurant workers. Have your children name sea-related jobs, and list each one on a sheet of chart paper. Then let each child choose one job, draw a picture to illustrate it, and print the job name under the picture. Bind the pages together to create a class book titled "Sea Jobs."

Endangered Species

Read aloud *Humphrey, The Lost Whale: A True Story* by Wendy Tokuda and Richard Hall. Talk about why the humpback whale is considered an endangered species. Then describe the steps being taken to preserve these valuable creatures.

Swimmy

Read aloud *Swimmy* by Leo Lionni. Ask your children to describe how the school of small fish solved a very big problem. Discuss the benefits of working cooperatively. Then have your youngsters work together to create an under-the-sea mural. Draw the ocean floor on the bottom of a large sheet of blue paper. Divide the class into small groups. Give each group a pattern for a starfish, fish, crab, sea anemone, or sea horse to trace and cut out. Then let the children work as a class to attach the various pieces to the sheet of background paper.

ART

Crayon Resist

A successful crayon-resist painting depends upon the following things: the paper used should be white or light-colored construction paper, the crayons must be very waxy (Prang crayons work well) and applied very heavily to the paper, and several layers of newspaper padding should be placed under the paper before coloring to ensure a solid application of crayon.

With these recommendations in mind, set up a center in the classroom where children can create crayon-resist paintings of life under the sea. Begin by allowing the children time to color their pictures. Then give each child a paintbrush and a small jar of blue, water-diluted tempera paint. Have each child dip her brush into the jar and carefully paint over the entire surface of her picture. The paint will color the areas of the paper not covered with crayon and will help create the illusion of an underwater scene.

One final note: As the paint begins to dry, the paper will curl. To remedy this situation, allow the paint to dry completely and place the paintings under heavy books to help straighten them.

Plaster Relief

An attractive plaster relief can be made using a variety of small seashells, several pie tins, and moist earth clay. First give each child in a learning center a pie tin and a ball of clay. Have her place the clay in the bottom of the tin, piece by piece, until the bottom is filled to a one-inch thickness. Next let her create impressions in the clay and pour liquid plaster over it until an approximate one-inch thickness is obtained. To make a hanger for the sculpture, insert a bent paper clip into the wet plaster. Finally allow the plaster to dry completely, and carefully separate it from the pie tin and the clay.

Diorama

Ask each child to bring a large shoebox lid from home. Then, in a small group, have each child paint the inside of her lid white. When the paint has dried completely, let her use markers to draw the ocean floor and some seaweed inside the lid. Next place a container of small, plastic fish, crabs, starfish, and sea horses in the learning center, and let each child choose four or five. Tell her to glue the objects to the sea scene. Then cover the lid with blue-tinted plastic wrap and tape the plastic to the back of the lid.

SNACK

Sand Cups

2 cups cold milk
1 package (4-serving size) Jell-O vanilla-flavor
  instant pudding
1 tub (8 oz.) Cool Whip whipped topping, thawed
1 package (12 oz.) vanilla wafers, crushed
8–10 (7 oz.) clear plastic cups
suggested decorations: miniature umbrellas;
  Gummy seashells, worms, and sharks; candy
  stars

Pour milk into large bowl. Add pudding mix. Beat with whisk until well blended, about 1 to 2 minutes. Let stand 5 minutes. Stir in whipped topping and half of crushed cookies. Place 1 tablespoon of crushed cookies into each cup. Fill cups three-fourths full with pudding mixture. Top with remaining crushed cookies. Refrigerate for 1 hour. Decorate as desired. Yield: 8–10 sand cups.

CULMINATING ACTIVITY

Beach Party

At the beginning of the week, send home a letter with each child explaining that a class beach party will be held on the last day of the Under the Sea unit. Encourage every child to bring to school an item that he might normally take with him to the beach (sand bucket, small plastic shovel, beach towel, sunglasses, etc.).

On the day of the party, let the children wear their beach apparel, and have several outside beach activities planned. For example, you may have the class participate in beach ball relay races, sand castle–building competition, or target practice with water guns. Afterwards, when you bring the children back into the classroom, allow them to rest on their beach towels, and play beach music in the background. Finally let the children enjoy a "sand cup" Jell-O pudding snack (see the recipe at left) before they go home. It will be a day that they will surely remember!

Name _____

Observing shells

Seashell Lab Sheet

	Yes	No
1. Did you see a shell with purple on it?	☐	☐
2. Did you see a shell that was shiny?	☐	☐
3. Did you see a shell that had ridges?	☐	☐
4. Did you see a shell with points?	☐	☐
5. Did you hear a sound in a shell?	☐	☐